"The Lord's Prayer is the most important teaching ever about talking with God. That's why it's a subject of universal and perennial interest to followers of Jesus. It's easy to learn yet infinitely profound. So many have thought so much and so deeply about it, yet no one writer can expound all its riches. Kevin DeYoung has added another helpful volume to the church's library on the prayer. His book is fresh without trying to be clever, contemporary without forgetting church history, and concise without being simplistic. It's exactly the kind of work we've come to expect from the pen of DeYoung and demonstrates why people find his preaching and writing so edifying."

Donald S. Whitney, Professor of Biblical Spirituality and Associate Dean, The Southern Baptist Theological Seminary; author, *Family Worship*; *Praying the Bible*; and *Spiritual Disciplines for the Christian Life*

"The Lord's Prayer is familiar to many of us, but how well do we really understand each phrase? Scholarly works on the Lord's Prayer can turn out to be surprisingly complex. Here is a clear, grace-filled, practical exposition that will benefit readers of all levels. DeYoung helps readers see the place of the Lord's Prayer in the context of all of Scripture and how it relates to Christ himself."

Brandon D. Crowe, Professor of New Testament, Westminster Theological Seminary

"As part of listening to a daily liturgy podcast, I pray the Lord's Prayer. I look forward to it as a highlight of each day, and it never feels like a ritual. Kevin DeYoung's book encourages me in my daily routine, ignites my passion for praying the Lord's Prayer, and solidifies my understanding of the petitions I gladly voice. The Lord's Prayer is clear and direct, concise and profound—so too is DeYoung's highly recommended book!

Gregg R. Allison, Professor of Christian Theology, The Southern Baptist Theological Seminary; author, *Sojourners and Strangers*; *Roman Catholic Theology and Practice*; and *Historical Theology*

T0026896

"Kevin DeYoung has given us a brief, encouraging, insightful look at the Lord's Prayer. He combines for us his own meditations and learning and adds some ideas about this prayer from the collective wisdom of the past. The result is what we would expect from this author: a pastoral, clear, simple (not simplistic), inspiring, and biblical teaching on the best-known prayer that ever came from the lips of our Lord. "

Miguel Núñez, Teaching Pastor, International Baptist Church of Santo Domingo, Dominican Republic; Founding President, Wisdom & Integrity Ministries

"In his exposition of the Lord's Prayer, DeYoung reminds us that a glorious vision of our God moves us to pray, and he explains the words of our Lord Jesus that we may know what to pray. Without limiting us to just one form, Kevin shows us that Jesus's model prayer provides the very foundation we need to sustain a vibrant life of communion with the living God in prayer. If you want to grow in prayer, take up and read. Then put it into practice."

Juan R. Sanchez, Senior Pastor, High Pointe Baptist Church, Austin, Texas; author, *The Leadership Formula*

"Even though one of the greatest privileges we have as Christians is to come to our heavenly Father in prayer, we often struggle to pray. *The Lord's Prayer* begins with how we should pray, expounds on what Jesus taught us to pray, and ends in a crescendo of God-exalting prayer. It will give you a sense of the greatness of the God who listens to our prayers, which will spur you on to pray. Read this book, then read it again with someone in your church."

Keri Folmar, Director of Women's Ministries, United Christian Church of Dubai; author, *The Good Portion: Scripture*

"Is it true that familiarity breeds contempt? I sure hope not, especially as it relates to the Lord's Prayer. Many Christians can recite this prayer of Jesus by heart, but they may not realize how helpful it can be to both jump-start and sustain their often inert prayer life. With his usual clarity and profundity, Kevin DeYoung walks us through the Lord's Prayer, revealing how it can be a foundation for all of our communion with God. So take up and read, because this book will help propel deeper faith in and stronger commitment to the gift that is prayer."

Julius J. Kim, President, The Gospel Coalition; Professor of Practical Theology, Westminster Seminary California

The Lord's Prayer

The Lord's Prayer

Learning from Jesus on What, Why, and How to Pray

Kevin DeYoung

FOUNDATIONAL TOOLS FOR OUR FAITH SERIES

WHEATON, ILLINOIS

The Lord's Prayer: Learning from Jesus on What, Why, and How to Pray
Copyright © 2022 by Kevin DeYoung
Published by Crossway
        1300 Crescent Street
        Wheaton, Illinois 60187

Published in association with the literary agency of Wolgemuth & Associates, Inc.

Cover design: Jordan Singer

First printing 2022

Printed in the United States of America

Trade paperback ISBN: 978-1-4335-5971-6
ePub ISBN: 978-1-4335-5974-7
PDF ISBN: 978-1-4335-5972-3
Mobipocket ISBN: 978-1-4335-5973-0

Library of Congress Cataloging-in-Publication Data

Names: DeYoung, Kevin, author.
Title: The Lord's prayer : learning from Jesus on what, why, and how to pray / Kevin DeYoung.
Description: Wheaton, Illinois : Crossway, 2022. | Series: Foundational tools for our faith | Includes bibliographical references and index.
Identifiers: LCCN 2021028858 (print) | LCCN 2021028859 (ebook) | ISBN 9781433559716 (trade paperback) | ISBN 9781433559723 (pdf) | ISBN 9781433559747 (epub) | ISBN 9781433559730 (mobipocket)
Subjects: LCSH: Lord's prayer. | Prayer—Christianity. | Jesus Christ—Teachings.
Classification: LCC BV230 .D49 2022 (print) | LCC BV230 (ebook) | DDC 226.9/6—dc23
LC record available at https://lccn.loc.gov/2021028858
LC ebook record available at https://lccn.loc.gov/2021028859

Crossway is a publishing ministry of Good News Publishers.

BP   31   30   29   28   27   26   25   24   23   22
15   14   13   12   11   10   9   8   7   6   5   4   3   2   1

To the faithful saints at Christ Covenant who
pray for their pastor without ceasing

Contents

1

When You Pray

IS THERE ANY ACTIVITY more essential to the Christian life, and yet more discouraging *in* the Christian's life, than prayer?

We know we should pray. We want to pray (or at least we want to want to pray). We admire those who do pray. And yet when it comes to actually praying, most of us feel like failures.

If someone asked us right now, "How is your prayer life going?" very few of us would be happy for the question and confident in our response. We wish we prayed more often. We wish we prayed longer. We wish we prayed better. I bet none of us anticipates getting to the end of our lives and thinking to ourselves, "You know what? I feel really good about what my prayer life has been all these years." We are much more apt to resonate with the question I read from a pastor several years ago as he reflected on his own life and prayer: "How can something I'm so bad at be God's will for my life?"

I've read a lot of books on prayer over the years. The best ones make me hopeful and grateful that God invites my prayers. Too many of the books, however, make even the most earnest Christian feel like a failure for doing anything else besides prayer. I remember reading a classic book on prayer early in my ministry. It was inspirational at first but deflating by the end. The problem may very well have been in my heart, but as I recall the book, it was a relentless exhortation to more committed prayer. In my experience, nonstop focus on the *ought* of prayer stirs up the Christian at first but quickly wears off, leaving in its wake more guilt than prayer. While there may be a short season where you say, "Yes, I'm going to pray more," over the long haul you just feel this low- to medium-grade guilt for not praying enough.

But the Lord's Prayer is different. It doesn't focus on the will to pray, at least not explicitly. The Lord's Prayer teaches us how to pray.

A Prayer for the Ages

It is hard to overstate the importance of the Lord's Prayer. Throughout church history, new converts and children have been discipled chiefly in three areas: the Apostles' Creed, the Ten Commandments, and the Lord's Prayer. For most of the last two millennia, it was assumed that if you were a Christian, you knew, memorized, and frequently prayed the Lord's Prayer.

In one sense, John 17 is more precisely the Lord's Prayer. It is the longest recorded prayer in Scripture from the Lord Jesus. What we know as the Lord's Prayer is not the prayer Jesus prayed (at least not exactly—how could he say, "Forgive us our debts"?), but the prayer he taught his disciples to pray.

There are two versions of the Lord's Prayer, one in Luke and the more familiar one in Matthew. I don't think one prayer is dependent upon the other. A simpler explanation is that Jesus, like any itinerant preacher, taught on the same things over and over, with different words and in slightly different ways.

In Luke 11:1–2 Jesus's teaching is prompted by the disciples' request, "Lord, teach us to pray" (v. 1). They must have heard something in the way Jesus was praying that made them think, "We have a lot to learn." Notice what Jesus did *not* talk about in response to their request. He didn't teach them how long their prayers should be, or at what time of day they should pray, or how many times each day they should pray, or what they should feel as they pray, or whether they should be standing or sitting or kneeling, or if they should close their eyes and fold their hands, or whether they should lift their hands and eyes to heaven.

It's not that concern about those things is wrong. But surely it's instructive that Jesus was most concerned with *what* they prayed, more than with when or where or for how long. This may be the most obvious and most important lesson to learn from Jesus about prayer. We can pray in the morning or in the evening, for a long time or a short time, with eyes open or eyes shut. There is freedom in a great many elements of prayer. But (1) we must not neglect praying, and (2) we must pray for the sort of things Jesus tells us to pray for.

The passage in Matthew 6:5–9 is part of Jesus's famous Sermon on the Mount (Matt. 5–7). You've probably realized that before. What you may not have noticed is that this section in the Sermon on the Mount covers the three foundational acts of Jewish piety: almsgiving (6:1–4), prayer (6:5–15), and fasting (6:16–18). These were the "spiritual disciplines" for first-century Jews (they would have memorized much of the Bible, but most couldn't read it daily because much of the population was illiterate, and individual families did not have Scripture scrolls in their homes). If they made New Year's resolutions back then, they would have thought of giving to the poor, praying, and fasting.

Unlike Jesus's teaching in Luke, here in Matthew Jesus is concerned not just with the *what* of prayer but with the *how* of prayer. Specifically, Jesus wants to make sure we are praying for the right reasons from the right heart. In fact, that is his central concern in discussing all three acts of piety. When you give to the needy, don't make a big deal out of it. When you pray, don't do it to look good. And when you fast, don't draw attention to yourself. Jesus understands the pride and vanity that dwell in every human heart. Being religious doesn't mean you no longer seek vainglory. In fact, being religious is one of the chief ways in almost every culture that men and women find ways to nurture their pride and their vanity. What better way to look impressive before others than to be *spiritually* impressive?

So don't think for a moment, "Well, I'm a Christian, I go to church, and I'm spiritual and religious. I'm not in danger of these things." Actually those realities may mean we are in particular danger.

Of Course We Pray

Before we get into those specifics, however, look at the first four words of Matthew 6:5: "And when you pray . . ." Jesus doesn't have to teach his disciples that they should pray. That was already a given. He assumed they would pray, and they would have understood that prayer was not something for super-spiritual people but something that every Jew did. Don't think, "Prayer is what pastors and missionaries do," or, "Prayer is something I will do when I'm older." Prayer is for everyone who is a true follower of God.

While it can be hard to know exactly when certain Jewish traditions developed, it seems clear that by the time of Jesus, prayer was offered in the synagogue three times a day.[1] This may have grown up out of Daniel's practice of praying three times a day (Dan. 6:10), or perhaps it goes back to Psalm 55:17: "Evening and morning and at noon I utter my complaint and moan, and he hears my voice." Typically, the time of synagogue prayer began with a recitation of the Shema (Deut. 6:4) followed by the Eighteen Benedictions. These benedictions are not in your Bible, but they deal with biblical themes. In fact, you can hear echoes in the Lord's Prayer of some of the language in them. These were a series of prayers asking God to bless Israel. We don't know exactly when they were codified, but the main development of the prayer almost certainly took place before the destruction of the temple in AD 70.[2]

If that's the case, Jesus and his disciples would have been familiar with these prayers. Jesus could assume not only that his disciples would have times of private prayer (like Jesus did), but more obviously that they would regularly attend times of corporate prayer (think of the words "our" and "us" in the Lord's Prayer). When someone asks, "How is your prayer life?" we probably think, "How am I doing with my daily devotionals first thing in the morning?" That's not bad. But Jesus's disciples probably thought of corporate gatherings where they came together and prayed. Think about the Lord's Prayer itself. There is not one example of a singular pronoun in the model prayer Jesus gave to his disciples.

No one—not Jesus, not his followers—questioned that God's people would pray. The same is no less true today. If you are a part of the family of God, you will talk to your Father. If you never talk to your earthly father (if he is alive), especially if you live in the same house, something is very dysfunctional. Of course we talk to God in prayer. He is our heavenly Father. You can't be a Christian and not pray. There is no such thing as a nonpraying Christian.

How Should We Pray?

We will get to the Lord's Prayer itself in the next chapter. That is the *what* of prayer. For this chapter, we need to focus on the *how*.

According to Jesus, there are two big no-no's when it comes to how we pray: don't be like the hypocrites, and don't be like the pagans. First, then, Jesus does not want us to be like hypocrites when we pray:

> When you pray, you must not be like the hypocrites. For they love to stand and pray in the synagogues and at the street corners, that they may be seen by others. Truly, I say to you, they have received their reward. But when you pray, go into your room and shut the door and pray to your Father who is in secret. And your Father who sees in secret will reward you. (Matt. 6:5–6)

Let's make sure we understand the word *hypocrite*. The Greek word *hypokrites* means "play actor." As a negative label, it means someone who puts on a mask and plays a part, someone who pretends to be something he is not. And that's very much the meaning of our English word *hypocrite*. Hypocrites profess to believe one thing but actually live a completely different way.

A well-known vegetarian who eats bacon every night, a loud opponent of the tobacco industry who smokes a pack of cigarettes a day, a champion of family values who sleeps with prostitutes—these are hypocrites. They pretend to be what they are not. And specifically, their pretense is for the applause and esteem of others.

Too often, Christians think of hypocrites as people who do one thing but feel another. But that's not hypocrisy. Hypocrites publicize one set of beliefs but live by a different set of beliefs. When you come to church but don't feel like it, that's more like faithfulness. When you do the right thing in your marriage even when you don't feel much in love, that's fidelity. I've heard too many times, "Pastor, I would be a hypocrite to stay in this marriage because I'm not in love anymore." Or, "I would be a hypocrite to come to worship when I don't feel like worshiping." Or, "I would be a hypocrite to pray since I'm not sure what I believe and feel distant." Doing what is right when you don't feel like doing what is right is maturity. Professing one thing in public but living a different way in private is hypocrisy.

We can clearly see what Jesus has in mind from Matthew 6:1: "Beware of practicing your righteousness before other people in order to be seen by them." That's what hypocrites do. They don't really love God. They don't really love the kingdom. They don't really love the hallowing of God's name. They love to pray in the synagogues and at the street corners. They love to be seen by others. Obviously, it's not wrong to pray in public. Jesus isn't trying to overthrow corporate worship or corporate prayer (cf. Matt. 18:19–20; Acts 4:24–30). When Jesus comes to 6:9 he assumes a corporate context for praying. He's warning against what is all too common in all of our hearts, perhaps in the pastor's heart more than in anyone else's: being religious in public more than being religious in private. Our prayer life should be like the iceberg in the ocean, with a great mass of spirituality under the surface that no one can see, rather than iceberg lettuce floating in the water, with all the vegetable on top and nothing under the surface. Our prayer life should be more than meets the eye.

Jesus gives a warning for all of us, but especially for pastors, elders, deacons, women's Bible study leaders, small-group leaders, and anyone engaged in public ministry. Beware of religious professionalism. Beware of saying all the right things when out of your house and doing all the wrong things inside your house. You may be able to fool people for an hour or two once a week on Sunday, but you're not fooling God, and you're not fooling the people who live closest to you. Beware of this kind of religious professionalism. Don't pray in order to be seen by people.

Instead, Jesus says, close the door and pray to be seen by God. Do you see how prayer is a matter of faith? Do we really believe God hears us when we pray? Do we believe that God sees us? Do we believe that he will reward us? But when we pray in secret, do we believe that there is a God who sees in secret and is listening? That takes faith. If you live for the praise of men, that's all you'll get. Jesus says, "Don't be a fool. Don't live your life for earthly applause when you can get heavenly applause." Who cares if people out there think you're impressive when you can have God smile upon you? Do you believe that the God in secret sees you and will reward you?

A few months ago my wife and I got one of those baby monitors with a video camera. Now we know why our two-year-old sleeps so late in the morning. He plays in his crib for two hours after we put him to bed. It's amazing to see what's he's really doing when he doesn't know we are watching. Now imagine you're a little seven-year-old boy, and you love your father. You look up to your father. You know your father takes care of you. And your father has a camera on every wall to see what you are doing. Wouldn't that make a difference in how you live your life—not just in not doing the wrong things, but in how you do the right things? The boy doesn't need to feel pressure to measure up to his friends. He doesn't have to put on a show. He doesn't have to pretend to be what he's not. He just needs to be the same person wherever he goes, because wherever he goes, his Father is watching—not, in this instance, to punish, but to reward! Live for the one you can't see, not for the ones you can see. Do not be a hypocrite.

Second, Jesus does not want us to be like the pagans when we pray:

> And when you pray, do not heap up empty phrases as the Gentiles do, for they think that they will be heard for their many words. Do not be like them, for your Father knows what you need before you ask him. (Matt. 6:7–8)

Jesus uses the word "Gentiles" in verse 7, but he isn't thinking of ethnicity. He's thinking of people who pray when they don't know the true God. Years ago I was in New York City with a group of Christians meeting with and listening to different religious leaders in the city. Among other things, we watched, with permission, from the sidelines, Hindu and Sikh rituals. I'm sure many people there were sincere in their beliefs, and we respect their right to worship as they see fit. We believe in religious liberty for all people.

And yet from a Christian perspective, I could see exactly what Jesus was talking about. I saw young men performing religious rituals for the onlookers, and the young men seemed barely interested in what they were doing. They were lighting candles or spreading incense or praying prayers on behalf of others. The point was simply that the ritual got done. The words were spoken and the phrases were repeated.

You can see the same thing all over the world. In most Muslim countries, what matters is simply that the rituals are performed. Just say the right words, facing the right way at the right time. Some Buddhist countries make use of prayer wheels. People put their prayers in a box and then spin it around again and again so that the prayers are multiplied. It's a ritual; it's mechanistic. According to Jesus, that's not at all what prayer is about. Prayer is not like voting online for your favorite player to make the Pro Bowl or the All-Star game, when fans press the button over and over to give their choice as many votes as possible.

To be sure, elsewhere Jesus urges us to pray and never give up (Luke 18:1–8), but persistent prayer is very different from babbling prayer. The word in Matthew 6:7 is *battalogeo*, which means to heap up empty phrases or to keep on babbling (NIV). The King James Version translates it as "vain repetitions." The Greek word is a kind of onomatopoeia, a word that sounds like what it is (e.g., oink, quack, splash, buzz). Stop the *bat-ta-lo-ge-o*, Jesus says. Don't be like the pagans who think that the mere act of uttering words is by itself pleasing to God. The goal in prayer is not the completion of some mechanical ritual.

Praying with empty phrases and meaningless words happens more often than we might think. It can happen in liturgical churches. Pastors can read their liturgical formulas, this very precise language that has been shaped over centuries and is so rich, with all the passion of an exhausted customer service representative reading the same script for the millionth time ("This call may be recorded for quality and training purposes. How are you doing today, Mr. DeYoung?"). We can say the Apostles Creed or the Lord's Prayer or a responsive reading like it's an out-of-body experience. It's all too common for these precious words to become rote, lifeless, and dull.

On the other hand, you can also pray with empty phrases and meaningless words in very casual churches that don't make use of liturgies. Worship leaders can offer up their prayers without any forethought and pile up phrases that don't make a lot of sense, or may even be heretical. "Oh, dear Lord, Father God, we praise for you dying on the cross for our sins, and we just ask, Holy Spirit, that you'd be with us today and snuggle us up under the blanket of your love." We can think that the more emotional our prayers, the more we pile on divine titles, the more God will hear us. John Stott calls this kind of prayer all lips, no mind, no heart.[3]

We don't have to impress God with our formulas or our spontaneity. He knows what we need before we ask (Matt. 6:8). We don't pray because God needs help running the universe. We don't pray to change God's mind. We pray because God has ordained means to accomplish his ends. He has arranged things so that he will give more grace to those who petition him for it. God doesn't need prayer, but he uses prayer just like he uses other means. He uses rain to grow the crops, sun to warm the earth, and food to strengthen the body. In the same way, God uses prayer to do his sovereign work. In prayer, we are not instructing God as much as we are instructing ourselves.

Notice again the motivation in 6:9, for the instruction in verse 8 is based on the one who sees in secret. Jesus hasn't yet taught his disciples what to pray for, but already we see how important it is that we know to whom we are praying. We aren't praying to a hotheaded coach or to a distant king or to an austere supervisor. We are praying to our heavenly Father. If you believe that he's a good Father, then you don't have to try to impress other people. You know God will take care of you. And if you believe he's a great Father, then you don't have to heap up empty words. You know that God already knows what you need. You don't get extra credit for adding extra words.

When I give seminary students an assignment, I have to give some kind of approximate word count or they won't know what sort of paper they are supposed to write. But I always tell them, "Don't go over! I don't want to read any more than I have to! And don't pad out the paper with fluff. Say what you need to say and then don't say anything else. I am grading you on what you are saying, not on the fact that you found a very long-winded way of saying it."

Be the One, Not the 450

Don't be a hypocrite when you pray, and don't be a pagan. Those are no-no's when it comes to prayer. This leads to one summarizing thought. You've heard this before, but you need to hear it again because it's true: prayer is not a formula. Prayer is not an incantation. Prayer is not a recipe. Prayer is a relationship.

Think of the difference between Elijah and the prophets of Baal (1 Kings 18:20–40). The 450 prophets of Baal called upon their god from morning until noon. Then after Elijah mocked them, they doubled their efforts. They cried out and cut themselves until they were covered in blood. The Bible tells us, "As midday passed, they raved on until the time of the offering of the oblation, but there was no voice. No one answered; no one paid attention" (18:29). When it was Elijah's turn, he spoke the covenant name of God and claimed a covenant relationship with God. "O LORD, God of Abraham, Isaac, and Israel, let it be known this day that you are God in Israel, and that I am your servant, and that I have done all these things at your word" (18:36). In other words, he prayed to the God who was actually there, he prayed to the God he knew personally, and he prayed to the God he trusted. And then he prayed in a short, straightforward prayer for God to hear his servant and for God to glorify himself. "Answer me, O LORD, answer me, that this people may know that you, O LORD, are God, and that you have turned their hearts back" (18:37).

I started this chapter by saying that some books on prayer reinforce that we ought to pray, but the most helpful books make us want to pray. I hope this chapter and this book are like that. Yes, we must pray. That is a command in the Bible, and more than that, it is an assumption in the Bible. But if we are going to move from "I should pray more" to "I can pray," we have to think of prayer in the right way. And at the heart of that right way is understanding that our God is not hard of hearing, and he is not hard of heart. Speak to him. Shoot straight with him. Be plain with him. You don't need to impress him. As your heavenly Father, he already loves you. You just need to show up and talk to him. That's the good news.

And the even better news is that when we do show up for prayer, our heavenly Father will be gladly waiting there, ready to hear us and eager to listen.

2

Our Father

WE COME NOW TO THE LORD'S PRAYER itself. Most of us are probably so familiar with it that we never stop to think what an amazing thing it is that we have this prayer. What if you had the opportunity to ask the greatest basketball coach of all time to teach you how to shoot a basketball? Or if you were able to ask the greatest chef to teach you how to cook? Or if you were to ask the greatest fighter pilot you know to teach you how to fly a plane? You'd be on the edge of your seat ready to hear what the expert has to say and then to put the advice and example into practice.

How much more should we be ready and eager to hear from Jesus. He is much more than an expert in prayer, and prayer is infinitely more important than any hobby or skill or vocation. Prayer is absolutely indispensable for the Christian. We can't live without it.

Some time ago I came upon a friend who was finishing a conversation with a Christian man who happened to be an astronaut. The astronaut had made multiple trips into space, so no doubt he had a good bit of knowledge about space stations. If you were going to go live in a space station for a few months, you'd welcome advice from the astronaut on how to breathe while in space. You'd be pretty interested in what he had to say, wouldn't you? There aren't many things more important than knowing how to breathe.

In the Christian life there aren't many things more important than knowing how to pray. How blessed we are that Jesus has left for us, for all time, this prayer. He didn't just tell us to pray; he gave us the perfect model for how we should pray. What could be more important than that? As the church father Cyprian said, "What praying to the Father can be more truthful than that which was delivered to us by the Son who is the Truth, out of his own mouth?"[1] Martyn Luther called the Lord's Prayer "the very best prayer that ever came to earth or that anyone would ever have thought up."[2] And John Calvin pointed to the privilege of saying the Lord's Prayer because in it "the only-begotten Son of God supplies words to our lips that free our minds from all wavering."[3] We don't have to wonder when we pray this prayer, or when we pray according to this prayer, if we're praying what God wants to hear, or what pleases him, or what is fruitful and profitable; we know it from Jesus himself.

In the Didache, one of the earliest nonbiblical sources we have from the early church, Christians are instructed to pray the Lord's Prayer three times a day (likely borrowing this pattern from the tradition of synagogue prayer). Of course, there is nothing in the Bible that commands us to say the Lord's Prayer thrice daily. Such a command would probably lead us right back to the vain repetition that Jesus warned against earlier in Matthew 6. But the exhortation in the Didache tells us that the Lord's Prayer was important from the earliest days of the church. Christians have always understood that this was not just another prayer. It is the prayer that teaches us how to pray every other prayer. Obviously we don't have to include these exact words or rigidly follow this structure in every prayer, yet every Christian prayer ought to be informed and shaped by the Lord's Prayer. This is our model, and it teaches us what to pray for and, just as importantly, to whom we are praying.

Simple Structure

Looking at the Lord's Prayer you can see it as a simple structure. There is an opening address followed by six petitions. It's important that we realize that the statements in the opening address are not ascriptions. They do not ascribe something to God, as in "Your name is holy!" or "Your kingdom is coming!" They are petitions. They ask God to do something. The first set of three requests focuses on *God's glory*—his name, his kingdom, and his will. The second set of three requests focuses on *our good*—our provision, our forgiveness, and our protection. Of course, the two sets cannot be separated. God is glorified as he gives us what we need, and when we ask for what we need, we must always do it with an eye to God being glorified. That's a helpful way to think of these two sets of petitions, God's glory and our good.

Following the six petitions, there is, in our traditional reciting of the prayer, a concluding ascription: "Yours is the kingdom and the power and the glory forever." As we will see when we come to those final phrases, we don't find this concluding ascription in newer English translations because it is not in the best Greek manuscripts. Even so, it does reflect biblical truth and biblical language. It is fine that we use that traditional ending, which has passed down to us from the King James Version, so long as we realize where it does (and does not) come from.

Our plan for this chapter is simple. We are going to move phrase by phrase, sometimes word by word, through the opening address and first petition.

A Family Affair

The first word of the prayer in our English translation is "Our" (6:9), but the first word in Greek is *pater*, father. Sometimes you'll hear the Lord's Prayer called "Paternoster," which comes from the first two words in the Latin version of the prayer. Interestingly, there is an old type of elevator called a paternoster that is found mainly in Europe. It has a number of wooden platforms that cycle up and down without stopping. In order to ride on the paternoster, you have to step on and step off as it moves. According to some people, the device is called a paternoster because the contraption resembles rosary beads. I was told the name came from people praying every time they dared to use the thing.

Matthew 6:9 is not about elevators (even if it is elevated speech!). Again, we are probably too familiar with the prayer to properly marvel at what it says. The God of the universe—the God who made the world out of nothing; the God of Abraham, Isaac, and Jacob; the God of the ten plagues and the Red Sea; the God of the glory cloud in the tabernacle; the God who shakes the cedars of Lebanon; the God who showed himself to Daniel as the great Ancient of Days; the God before whom no one can stand face to face and live—Jesus wants us to call this God "Father."

To pray with intimacy to God as father is not a human right; it is a spiritual privilege. It is a privilege for the people of God who have been born again by the Spirit of God. "To all who did receive him, who believed in his name, he gave the right to become children of God, who were born, not of blood nor of the will of the flesh nor of the will of man, but of God" (John 1:12–13). It is not our natural human birthright to call God "Father"; it is our born-again spiritual birthright.

Granted, there is a sense in which one could say that God is father to all, insofar as all people owe their existence to God (Acts 17:28–29). But that's never how Jesus speaks of God the Father. One book I read made the old liberal argument about the universal fatherhood of God: "He is the father of all men." As proof of that point, the author cites not a single Bible verse but quotes Rudolf Bultmann.[4] There is no biblical warrant for thinking that God is father to all and that we are all his children in a spiritual sense.

Only disciples get to call God "Father." Even in the Old Testament, where the fatherhood of God is less clear than in the New Testament, we see that this intimate relationship of a father and his children is the special privilege reserved for God's people. Fifteen times the Old Testament uses *father* in a religious sense. But in the New Testament it is used 245 times. What was occasionally present in the Old Testament has become central in the New Testament, namely, that by God's initiative we can approach God as our father. "See what kind of love the Father has given to us, that we should be called children of God" (1 John 3:1).

Incidentally, but importantly, we cannot substitute "Mother" for "Father." Yes, the Bible sometimes describes God with maternal characteristics, e.g., tender like a nursing mother (Isa. 49:15) or like a hen brooding over her young (Matt. 23:37). We don't have to be embarrassed using those same sort of images, but that is not at all the same as naming God as mother. God is spirit, and he doesn't have a body. He does not have a biological gender; he's not male or female. Throughout Scripture he reveals himself as a king, a husband, and a father but never as a queen, a wife, or a mother. We have no warrant to pray to God in ways we may think sound better, are more culturally attuned, or our world thinks are more appropriate. The act of naming is an inherent act of authority (think of God naming Adam, and Adam naming Eve). We would be greatly presumptuous to think that we could give God a new identity and a new name without doing violence to revelation and usurping God's divine prerogatives (Ex. 3:13). This is not about the superiority of men over women; it is simply the way in which God has chosen to reveal himself, with masculine pronouns and titles.

To call on God as father is a gift of the triune God. It may look like prayer involves only the first person of the Trinity, but Romans 8 tells us that it is the Spirit of God who enables us to cry, "Abba! Father!," bearing witness that we are children, heirs of God, and fellow heirs with Christ (vv. 14–17). Anyone who truly prays the Lord's Prayer from the heart is demonstrating the work of the glorious Trinity. In union with God the Son, God the Spirit works in our hearts so that we call out in faith to God the Father.

The biggest indicator of *Christian* prayer (because, after all, lots of people pray) is not the geographic direction in which we pray, or the body position while we pray, or even that we experience a certain feeling when we pray. What makes it Christian prayer is, first, an awareness of the one to whom we pray. God doesn't want or need or delight in the mere repetition of words and phrases. He delights to hear from his children, to know that we love him, that we want to be with him, that we trust him, that we believe he cares for us, that we know he can do anything about everything. What we need when we pray is less awareness of ourselves and more awareness of God. When I get distracted or discouraged in prayer, I have to remind myself of the simple fact that someone is there, someone is listening, and not just anyone, but my Father who is in heaven. When I pray, I'm not going through a spiritual soliloquy, a ritual for the day, or something important to check off before I go to work; I am speaking to my Father and my God.

Remember who you are talking to in prayer. Jesus puts the prayer into the most intimate family terms. It's not, first, about proper protocol; when we know to whom we are talking, the right approach will follow. He's not your roommate or your butler or your girlfriend, so don't be chummy or demanding or romantic. But neither are we told to pray to him as a dictator, a parole officer, or a harsh taskmaster, like we have to plead with him against his better judgment to listen to us. So don't grovel, don't squirm, and don't be afraid. Come to him as a child, comforted that your Father loves you and confident that he wants to hear from you.

A Community Prayer

I just said that you should be confident that God wants to hear from you in prayer. More accurately, I should have said that he wants to hear from *us*, because, as I noted above, the first word in the prayer is *our*. Of course, we should pray by ourselves too. Jesus talked earlier about praying behind closed doors, and Jesus regularly modeled getting away in private for prayer (Matt. 14:23;

Mark 1:35; Luke 5:16). But it's striking that there is no first-person pronoun in the whole prayer. And this is the model prayer for all our praying. Even when we are praying alone, we are, in a sense, praying with the larger body of Christ. But I don't think that's mainly what Jesus has in mind in beginning the prayer with *our*.

The most important takeaway from *our* is that prayer is a corporate event. That's harder for us than it would have been for those in Jesus's day. Unless you live in a very tight-knit neighborhood or a dorm at a Christian college, most of us aren't gathering in small groups to pray every day. And yet wouldn't it be easier to be faithful in prayer if we weren't doing it alone? It does count if we are with other people! It's a good reason to pray as husband and wife, to do family worship at home, to join a small group, to gather with other believers at work, or to think about how to foster this sort of community at church. We should hear prayer and think, "That's what I get to do with other believers on a regular basis."

Jesus assumes that the prayer the disciples will pray will be with other Christians. He also assumes that as we pray in corporate settings, much of what we pray will be through familiar forms of prayer. Most of us in the evangelical tradition assume that real prayer is more or less extemporaneous or spontaneous. To be sure, there is something important about being able to pray in our own words, but let's not neglect the riches God has given us to use, such as a confession; a hymnal; the Book of Common Prayer; or *The Valley of Vision*, a book of Puritan prayers. There are so many resources, and we should not be afraid to use them. Jesus and his disciples were almost certainly familiar with the Eighteen Benedictions and could have recited them. When Jesus was in his greatest moment of trial on the cross, what came out of his mouth? Scripture utterances and Scripture prayers. When the disciples went out to sing prayers on the night of Jesus's betrayal, they sang the Hallel psalms (Psalms 113–118). When Jonah was in the belly of a fish, he prayed from Psalm 42:7, "All your waves and billows have gone over me." We can pray with freedom and with forms.

No Drab Deity

"Our Father *in heaven* . . ." (Matt. 6:9). It's precious to talk to one's father, but the amazing thing about Jesus's prayer is that our Father is in heaven. The amazement goes in both directions: God is my Father, and my Father is God! Many kids go through the phase of thinking that their dad is invincible. "My dad is so strong. My dad is so tall. My dad is so smart. My dad is so fast." But more importantly, "My God is so big, so strong, and so mighty—there's nothing my God cannot do."

Granted, the fatherhood of God is challenging for some. Some Christians grew up with a lame father, an abusive father, or no father at all. We can sympathize with those for whom the word *father* stirs up all sorts of bad connotations. But it's not like no one had poor experiences with their father in earlier centuries. Our Father in heaven is what earthly fathers should be like. We must interpret our experiences through God's revelation and not the other way around. The Father who loves us is the King who reigns over everything. "Our Father in heaven" tells us that we are praying to a God of intimacy and authority, and both are essential.

A quotation I read from J. I. Packer's book on the Lord's Prayer really stopped me in my tracks: "The vitality of prayer lies largely in the vision of God that prompts it. Drab thoughts of God make prayer dull."[5] I can't help but think about my own prayer life. Yes, we all struggle with distractions. We all struggle with discipline at times. We don't need to beat ourselves up when prayer is hard. It is for most of us. But if prayer usually feels dull and boring, I have to conclude that in large part I've lost a sense of who it is I'm praying to.

Think about people in your life whom you have loved praying with. When I think about those men and women in my own life, I think about the way that they were banging on the gates of heaven, how they prayed with a sense of awe and intimacy toward God, how they prayed to a big God who loved them and could act and was listening. I love to pray with that sort of person. When our prayers are dull and boring, might it be because our conception of God is dull and boring? If we knew who it was we were talking to, how could we not be eager to converse with him?

Drab thoughts of God make prayer dull. So get a better, truer, bigger, sweeter understanding of God, and see what that does to your prayer life.

That the World May Know

All we have covered is by way of the opening address. Now, finally, we get to the first petition: "Hallowed be your name" (6:9). Praying that God's name be hallowed does not mean that God's name could be holier. Glorifying God isn't like using a microscope, making small things look bigger; it's like using a telescope, bringing into view things that are unimaginably big. To hallow means, "May all the world and all created things see God for who he is, and may his human creatures, especially, adore and obey him." As Calvin puts it: "We would wish God to have the honor he deserves; men should never think of him without the highest reverence."[6]

There's a reason that this is the first petition—it is the one that holds all the others together. It puts all the others in focus and in the right ordering. If your children came to you and said, "We have several requests for you, but before we give you any of our requests, we want you to know that we love you, and whatever you do, we want you to be honored," then you would know something about the nature of all their subsequent requests.

The name of God is the sum of all the attributes and works of God. That's why the psalmist says that God has exalted above all things his name and his word (Ps. 138:2). It's why the Old Testament so often speaks of God acting for his name's sake (Ps. 25:11; Isa. 43:6–7; Ezek. 20:14; 36:22). According to the Heidelberg Catechism:

> "Hallowed be your name" means to bless, worship, and praise you for all your works and for all that shines forth from them: your almighty power, wisdom, kindness, justice, mercy, and truth. And it means, help us to direct all our living—what we think, say, and do—so that your name will never be blasphemed because of us but always honored and praised. (Lord's Day 47)

To pray this prayer is to ask that God would do a miracle in our hearts, in our actions, and in our world, that his name would be set apart. It makes plain to God our chief desire: to praise him and want all peoples to praise him. It's to want the whole world to see him for who he really is.

Whether it's our children, our spouse, a movie we like, or a painting we're fascinated by, we want people to come to appreciate all that we appreciate. We can learn a lot about people by what they ask for in prayer. So when we pray, "Our Father in heaven, hallowed be your name," we're saying, "O, God, may all the peoples praise you. Start with me, that I would know in my heart, and multiply it around the world." That's what we ask. That's the first thing we want from God in prayer.

This is the request that shapes every other request. This is the petition that supersedes all other petitions. Everything else follows from this supplication. We don't want to pray about our silly little empires. It's about God's name, not our name. Is there anything more countercultural than that request? Anything more radical? Anything more freeing?

To pray that way means glory for God, and it means goodness for us. The two cannot be separated. What is the chief end of man? The Westminster Shorter Catechism says that man's chief end is to glorify God and enjoy him forever. Those are not two goals but one chief end, because the two go together. The happiest life is the one lived for God's glory. So why would we want to pray for anything less?

3

Our Desire

FOR THE PAST FEW MONTHS, I've been making my way through Andrew Roberts's 1,100-page biography of Winston Churchill. It's an amazing book about an amazing life. One of the themes running throughout the book is Churchill's lifelong belief in the goodness and greatness of the British Empire. Roberts remarks that today we think differently of imperialism and colonialism and acknowledge many of the evils they perpetrated, but Churchill did not see things that way. When he experienced for the first time British rule in India, he admired the railways, the irrigation projects, the mass education, the newspapers, the bridges, roads, and aqueducts, the universities, the hospitals, the rule of law, the military protection afforded by the British army and navy, the benefits of the English language, and the abolition of traditional practices like burning widows on funeral pyres. For Churchill, this was all confirmation for what he was taught as an English aristocrat; namely, that Britain was worth living and dying for.

I am not interested here in the historical debate about the blessings and the curses of British rule in India. What I want us to notice is what Roberts says about the commitments Churchill embraced as a young man in his early twenties while stationed in India: "[Churchill] took the firm and irrevocable decision to dedicate his life to the defense of the British Empire against all its enemies, at home and abroad. Time and again throughout his political career, he would put his allegiance to his ideal of the Empire before his own best interests."[1]

If Winston Churchill, and so many other men and women like him of that age, could make that sort of commitment to the British Empire with all its evils and imperfections, how much more should we as Christians be committed to a vastly more gracious, more significant, and more eternal kingdom? What if it was said about you long after you were dead and gone that you took the firm and irrevocable decision to dedicate your life to the proclamation of the kingdom of God and its advancement against all its enemies, at home and abroad, and that time and again, you put your allegiance to God and his will above your own best interests? And ultimately, of course, the two don't diverge. Your best interests—my best interests—are in God's kingdom. Seek first that kingdom, and all these things will be added unto you (see Matt. 6:33). So, again, if Churchill could be committed to the British Empire, how much more ought we to be committed in our whole lives, with sacrifice and with zeal, to God's kingdom?

We are going to look, in this chapter, at the second and third petitions of the Lord's Prayer: "Your kingdom come, your will be done, on earth as it is in heaven" (Matt. 6:10). I have three questions. First, what is meant by God's kingdom and by God's will in this prayer? Second, what are we asking for when we make these two petitions? Third, how should we live our lives in light of these requests?

What Do We Mean?

First, what is meant by God's kingdom and by God's will in this prayer? This will be our longest point and require the most heavy lifting. Let's start with the word *kingdom*.

The Greek word for kingdom (*basileia*) occurs 162 times in the New Testament, so clearly this is an important biblical term. Although the Lord's Prayer uses the word *kingdom* as a stand-alone term, it is obviously a reference to God's kingdom. Any correct understanding of kingdom in the New Testament must emphasize that it is the kingdom of *God*. Matthew's Gospel often calls it the "kingdom of heaven," but that is simply a Jewish way of referring to the kingdom that belongs to the God who dwells in heaven.

A simple definition is to think of the kingdom of God as his reign and rule. Another way to think of the kingdom is as God's redemptive presence coming down from heaven to earth.

We can trace this theme throughout the Bible. God's presence, his holiness, and his covenant relationship were with Adam and Eve in the garden, and then because of sin and rebellion, they were kicked out of the garden, out of the earthly dwelling place of God's kingdom.

Then God promised a holy land. As we see throughout Genesis, his people looked forward to that land of Canaan. It was supposed to be a type of the garden of Eden. Its descriptions have echoes of the garden of Eden. Why was Canaan said to be a land flowing with milk and honey when, if you know anything about Israel, it's not flowing with a lot of milk or honey? It's a pretty hard place to make a living by farming, but it was described with images of abundance because it was evocative of the garden. This was the promised land that God had made for them, where he would dwell in their midst, with the tabernacle and then with the temple, and they would be gathered around his presence.

Eventually, because of sin and rebellion, God's people were kicked out of the promised land and exiled to Babylon. Once again, God's people were sent east of Eden.

Over time they were allowed to return to Canaan and build a new temple. But when Jesus came, he announced that he would be the new temple, a new Israel, indicating that God's presence on earth would no longer be situated around a land or a building but around a person. So now the redemptive presence of God is experienced in the church. The church—like the garden of Eden and ancient Israel—is the place where God's laws are established, where his presence is known, and where the heavenly realities of love and forgiveness and salvation are meant to be experienced. And the Old Testament language of lawbreakers being put outside the camp or being punished physically is now appropriated in the New Testament to mean church discipline. God's people today are not physically put to death, but like those in Eden and Israel, if you prove to be wicked and unbelieving, they are put outside the camp.

It is important to say something here about the relationship between the kingdom and the church. The two are not identical, but they cannot be separated, and in this life, they largely overlap. We can think of the church as a kind of outpost or embassy of the kingdom. An embassy is a national outpost situated in a foreign land. The embassy, while it wants to dwell peacefully in the foreign land, exists to advance the interests of another country. Likewise, the church—dwelling on earth in various nations around the world—exists to advance the interests of another kingdom, a heavenly kingdom. The church is the place where you expect to see the values and rules of the kingdom honored and upheld. The church is supposed to be the outpost of heaven on earth, which is why the poor should be provided for *in the church* and why the wicked and unbelieving don't belong *in the church*. The reason the church in its mission is not about societal transformation is the same reason the church does not throw sinners into the lake of fire. The heaven on earth we seek to create is the heavenly reality among God's people in the church. Yes, we believe in a heaven on earth, but not in a utopian scheme of transforming society writ large. History is littered with bad example after bad example of people who thought they could create heaven on earth. Human attempts to create heaven on earth have killed millions.

Life in the church looks forward to the eternal life where God's redemptive presence will be enjoyed to the fullest. In the age to come, the kingdom will no longer be something that has broken in here or there; it will be all in. Think of the good news from Revelation 11:15, which you may have heard in Handel's *Messiah*: "The kingdom of this world has become the kingdom of our Lord and of his Christ, and he shall reign forever and ever." That's what's coming. The kingdom of God is the heavenly world breaking into our earthly existence. Do not think of the kingdom as a realm to which we are going as much as a reality that is coming to us. The kingdom reveals both the meaning and the goal of history.

From this brief survey of redemptive history, we can see that the kingdom is both present and future.

Already and Not Yet

In one sense, Jesus is already King. In another sense, he needs to become King. The kingdom of God can refer to the age to come:

> When the Son of Man comes in his glory, and all the angels with him, then he will sit on his glorious throne. Before him will be gathered all the nations, and he will separate people from one another as a shepherd separates the sheep from the goats. And he will place the sheep on his right, but the goats on the left. Then the King will say to those on his right, "Come, you who are blessed by my Father, inherit the kingdom prepared for you from the foundation of the world." (Matt. 25:31–34)

That is the kingdom that is coming. It's the age to come, the heavenly reward.

Similarly, in Matthew 13 Jesus says the Son of Man will send his angels to gather out of his kingdom all causes of sin and all lawbreakers and throw them into the fiery furnace. Then the righteous will shine like the sun in the kingdom of their Father (Matt. 13:41–43). That's the age to come. And Jesus says in John 18:36 that his kingdom is not of this world, meaning that he did not come to rule from an earthly throne and that his kingdom had not yet been established.

Clearly, then, the kingdom, in one sense, is *coming*. But in another sense, it *has come*. We won't make sense of the New Testament until we get these two things in our head: the kingdom has come and is coming. Jesus says, "If it is by the Spirit of God that I cast out demons, then the kingdom of God has come upon you" (Matt. 12:28). It's present. In Luke 17:21 Jesus tells the Pharisees they are looking for the kingdom in the wrong ways by expecting an observable king like they had experienced in the past. "The kingdom of God," Jesus says, "is in the midst of you." Now that's an audacious thing to say. If I went around saying, "The kingdom is right here in the midst of you because I'm here," that would be a good reason for my church to make me their former senior pastor. But Jesus can say it because it's true. Where he is, where the King is, there the kingdom has come. And Colossians 1:13 says believers have been delivered from the domain of darkness and transferred into the kingdom of God's beloved Son.

The kingdom is already and not yet. It is present and future. It is like the sun in the sky breaking through the clouds, but the rain has not fully passed and the brightness of the sun is not now experienced as it will be in the future. This is why Jesus tells so many parables with the same basic point: the kingdom looks small and unimpressive right now, but at the end of the age it will be unbelievably grand and glorious.

I'm belaboring this point because "kingdom" is one of those areas over which well-meaning Christians can get their theology sideways. We need to be on our guard against certain misunderstandings about the kingdom of God. Think about the apostles in Acts 1. Jesus has risen from the dead and is about to ascend into heaven. And as the disciples are gathered together, they ask one final question of Jesus: "Lord, will you at this time restore the kingdom to Israel?" (1:6). They say there are no bad questions, but this one came close. The disciples show once again that they do not fully understand what sort of messiah Jesus is and what sort of kingdom he brings. They also misunderstand the timing of the kingdom. They think it is all present ("at this time"), when it is present and future. That is why the Acts passage concludes, "This Jesus, who was taken up from you into heaven, will come in the same way as you saw him go into heaven" (1:11).

They misunderstand the domain of the kingdom. They are still thinking of a national kingdom for Israel, when Jesus is talking about a universal kingdom. Membership in this dominion is not by ethnic heritage or geography. You enter by faith and repentance, and it is available and extended to all who will enter by faith and repentance. This is why Jesus again corrects their thinking in Acts 1:8, saying in effect, "It's too small a thing for me to restore an earthly kingdom to Israel. You will be my witnesses in Jerusalem and Judea, in Samaria, and to the ends of the earth." This is not a kingdom for Israel; it is a universal kingdom.

Most fundamentally, they misunderstood the nature of the kingdom. They thought it was political and earthly, when it was spiritual and heavenly. All throughout the Gospels, people were expecting Jesus to marshal an army, throw off the Romans, and establish a literal and obvious throne. But the good news of the kingdom would not be good news to Gentiles in Ephesus or Rome if it were a message about an earthly throne in Jerusalem. No, it's about a universal, heavenly, spiritual kingdom. The violent tried to take the kingdom of heaven by force (Matt. 11:12), but Jesus said, no one can see the kingdom unless he is born again (John 3:3). Over and over, he's correcting their misunderstanding about the nature of the kingdom. "You are thinking that this comes by earthly means; it doesn't. It comes by the Spirit of God."

We cannot bring about the kingdom by elections or education or humanitarian good works or environmental stewardship or by the cultivation of the arts. This is where we must not be confused. Yes, kingdom values should infiltrate our politics. Kingdom living should make a difference in our communities. But let us not misunderstand the nature of the kingdom. The kingdom does not advance when trees are planted, or unemployment lowered, or beautiful art is created, or elections go one way or another. Those may all be important things. They may reflect certain values of the kingdom. But the kingdom comes when and where the King is known. When Jesus is loved and worshiped and believed upon, there the kingdom of God is in the midst of you.

We also need to understand what Jesus means by *the will of God*. Just as there were ways to think of the kingdom both as present and future and as coming and having come, there are two aspects to the will of God in Scripture. We can think of these two sides of the same coin as God's will of decree and God's will of desire. God's will of decree refers to God's sovereign sway over all things, what he has determined in eternity past. In this sense, everything that comes to pass is according to the will of God, and nothing comes to pass except as it conforms to the will of God:

- Are not two sparrows sold for a penny? And not one of them will fall to the ground apart from your Father. But even the hairs of your head are all numbered. (Matt. 10:29–30)

- In him we have obtained an inheritance, having been predestined according to the purpose of him who works all things according to the counsel of his will. (Eph. 1:11)

So, according to Scripture, God's will of decree is that which cannot be thwarted, that which is already fixed from eternity past.

But we can also think of God's will in Scripture as his will of desire, that is, what he commands of us and wants from us as we follow him:

- Not everyone who says to me, "Lord, Lord," will enter the kingdom of heaven, but the one who does the will of my Father who is in heaven. (Matt. 7:21)

- Do not love the world or the things in the world. If anyone loves the world, the love of the Father is not in him. For all that is in the world—the desires of the flesh and the desires of the eyes and pride in possessions—is not from the Father but is from the world. And the world is passing away along with its desires, but whoever does the will of God abides forever. (1 John 2:15–17)

We see in verses like these that the will of God is shorthand for obedience to God's commands and walking in his way. Doing the will of God means we say no to the desires of the flesh, the desires of the eyes, and pride in possessions. In this sense, we can submit to the will of God or not. The will of God in these passages does not refer to the way God ordains things but to the way God commands us to live. This is the type of will we are praying about in the Lord's Prayer. The difference between earth and heaven is not that God is sovereign over heaven but not over earth. The difference is that every command is fulfilled with cheerful and full obedience in heaven, where that is not the case here on earth.

Incidentally, what we usually mean when we want to know the will of God is a will of direction. That's another topic that I won't elaborate on here, except to say that there is no will of direction that God *means for us to discover ahead of time*. He guides and directs all our steps. He may even surprise us with supernatural leading that won't make sense until after the fact, but nowhere in the New Testament are we commanded to seek out a mysterious will of direction whereby God tells us what to do at every fork in the road. What is important to God is that we rest in his will of decree, we obey his will of desire, and we trust that he is directing our lives through wisdom and good counsel, even when he doesn't show us the exact next step to take.

So all of that is to say, when we pray about the will of God in the Lord's Prayer, we are talking mainly about God's will of desire: "May your commandments be done, and all that you desire for your creatures be done here on earth as it is in heaven."

What Are We Praying For?

Second, what are we asking for when we make these two petitions? When I was in college I kept a prayer journal. It's amazing how having a whole bunch of kids gives you much less time for self-reflection. After my freshman year, I tallied up all the things I had prayed for just to reflect on what I was spending all my time praying about. Three prayer concerns came up over and over again: (1) A family member who had been struggling with some physical issues. (2) Girls, because I always had internal drama about some girl I liked. (3) Running, because I wanted to be a great runner. These were the three things I prayed about over and over. Now were those bad things to pray about? No. I wasn't praying for assassinations or for a life of crime. I was casting all my cares on the Lord, which is good. But my prayers weren't exactly centered on Jesus's priorities. I was not praying big, God-centered, kingdom-focused prayers.

You should not feel shame in bringing before the Lord the smallest things. You can't find your car keys? You want your dog to get better? Cast your cares on the Lord. But recognize that it doesn't take the Spirit of God to want those things. You don't have to be a Christian to want sick people to get better. You don't have to be a Christian to want a job or to get married or to have kids, to have your life go well.

When we pray, "Heavenly Father, your kingdom come and your will be done, on earth as it is in heaven," we are asking God for the in-breaking of the messianic age. We are asking for his commandments to be obeyed promptly, gladly, and sincerely. We are asking for Christ to reign in human hearts. We are asking for the redemptive presence of God to be known and felt here and now. We are asking for the reign and rule of heaven to be experienced on earth. We are asking for God's final victory to arrive sooner than we think. The Lord's Prayer is the cry of God's people saying, "Come, Lord Jesus, come quickly." To pray this petition, D. A. Carson writes, is "to ask that God's saving, royal rule be extended now as people bow in submission to him and already taste the eschatological blessing of salvation and to cry for the consummation of the kingdom."[2] Is that what is uppermost in your prayer life and mine?

Later in Matthew 6, Jesus will tell his disciples to seek first the kingdom of God and his righteousness (v. 33). The kingdom of God may not be the only thing you ever care about. You care about a sports team, you care about food, you care about a movie or entertainment. These aren't necessarily bad things, but they become very bad things if they become first things. And that means we must not allow any other identity to cut in line ahead of our identity as children of our heavenly Father and citizens of a heavenly kingdom. We do not seek first the advancement of people with our skin color, whatever that skin color may be. We do not seek first the advancement of Western civilization, though I give thanks for it and want people to learn about it. We do not seek first the triumph of our political party or even of our nation. We seek first God's kingdom, and we pray that his kingdom would come, whatever it may mean for our personal, tribal, and earthly kingdoms. We must always get the order and the priority right—God's kingdom first. That is our ultimate identity and concern.

Before we move to the third and final question, notice one more important thing. In the New Testament, we see God's people praying for the kingdom and proclaiming the kingdom, but we never see the language that they are *building* the kingdom. Pay attention to the verbs associated with the kingdom of God. The kingdom can come, it can arrive, it can appear. But we do not establish the kingdom, expand the kingdom, or grow the kingdom. The kingdom of God is not a society to be built but a gift to be received.

It is again like the sun breaking in. You don't build the sun. You don't make the sun. You can pray that the clouds would part. You can declare to people the rays and the warmth of the sun, but it's not something you can build or bring. The kingdom is *God's* kingdom, and we can receive it, seek it, enter it, or inherit it, but we do not create it, bring it, or even give it to others. Only God can give the kingdom (Luke 12:32). In praying these petitions in the Lord's Prayer, we are not laying down a blueprint for cultural renewal or societal transformation, though that may happen as we try to live faithfully. We are praying for a miracle of God's regenerating power and redemptive grace.[3]

How Then Should We Live?

Third, and finally, how should we live in light of these requests? We live obediently, outwardly, and expectantly.

Obediently

We must always remember that Christian prayer isn't ultimately a way to make God do our will. That's paganism or magic. There's nothing Christian about that. Who doesn't want an all-powerful being to be at our beck and call? Who wouldn't want a genie in a lamp? No, do not pray that God would do our will. In Christian prayer we ask that the world and everything and everyone would be conformed to God's will. That's mature Christian faith, and that's what Christian prayer sounds like.

Think of the first three petitions: for God's name, God's kingdom, and God's will. We pray to our heavenly Father, "May you work in such a way that the world will glorify your name, submit to your reign, and follow your rule." It's a big prayer—it's bigger than what most of us tend to pray—and done rightly, it is a humble prayer. As J. I. Packer reminds us, "To pray 'thy kingdom come' is searching and demanding, for one must be ready to add, 'and start with me; make me your fully obedient subject.'"[4]

Isn't that true? It's one thing to pray, "God, your kingdom come; your will be done; there's a lot of bad guys out there, and they need to be changed." But if we have a Christian heart, a born-again heart, we think, "O, Lord, would you start with me? Would you start with us? Would you start with our church? Would you show us our disobedience?" So we pray and look obediently.

Outwardly

We can't bring the kingdom or build the kingdom, but we can announce the kingdom. "What Judaism had believed would come all at once is split into two parts, with a mission in between."[5] The very first thing Jesus says in Mark is the singular message of his entire public ministry: "Now after John was arrested, Jesus came into Galilee, proclaiming the gospel of God, and saying, 'The time is fulfilled, and the kingdom of God is at hand; repent and believe in the gospel'" (Mark 1:14–15). Jesus's mission was saving sinners, and his method was proclamation. Jesus never entered a town and set up a healing clinic or an exorcism ministry. To be sure, he also healed the sick and cast out demons, but the reason he came out in public ministry was to preach (1:38). The presence of the kingdom is marked by the advancement of the gospel. If you care about the kingdom coming, you will care about the advancement of the gospel.

That's what we see throughout the book of Acts. The word *kingdom* appears seven times, each of which has to do with some new advance for the gospel or some new proclamation of the gospel (importantly, the book begins and ends with bearing witness and the kingdom: 1:6; 28:31). The spread of God's reign and rule does not come by armies or elections but by the Spirit of God working through the words of the apostles and their followers.

Some of you will be the answer to your own prayers. You may be the answer to other people's prayers. When we pray, "Father, your kingdom come," we are asking God to send people out to the uttermost parts of the earth, "proclaiming the kingdom of God and teaching about the Lord Jesus Christ will all boldness and without hindrance" (Acts 28:31). The kingdom is entirely of God and from God. The harvest is in his hands. But he gives us seed to sow. And wherever we are in our own Jerusalem or Judea, let us be faithful to sow those seeds, to have a personal witness and a church that is outward-facing. You can't pray, "Your kingdom come and your will be done" without thinking about the advancement of the gospel.

Expectantly

We do not pray as those who have no hope. God is mighty to save. It takes faith to pray. Throw out your prayers as a protest against the status quo of sin and sadness. Trust in the Lord and his promises. Blessed are the poor in the spirit, for theirs is the kingdom of heaven (Matt. 5:3). Blessed are those who are persecuted for righteousness' sake, for theirs is the kingdom of heaven (5:10). Do you want the kingdom of God in you, among you? It comes to the poor in spirit. It comes to those who are persecuted for righteousness' sake. Churchill was right—some empires are worth living and dying for. It just so happens that there's an empire, a kingdom, that's of eternally more significance than the British Empire, or the United States of America, or any earthly nation.

Believe that the Lord is a judging God. This expectation should spur us to speak (Acts 20:26–27) and move us to pray. Believe also that he is an inviting God. There is a feast to come, a banquet, a wedding celebration. And the God of the universe is sending out invitations, and by his grace, some of those people will receive it. Some will throw it in the trash; some will say, "Not interested"; some will be angered; and some will say, "What is this about?" Maybe it will take seven or ten or twenty times to read that invitation before they say, "You know what? I want to be at that feast. I want to be a part of that banquet. I want to be in that kingdom." The God of the universe is inviting people, going into the highways and byways, and inviting all the rabble, just like us, to come to his wedding feast. Let us trust that some will be glad for the invitation, and some will be gathered around the banqueting table because we sent, we went, we spoke, and we prayed.

4

Our Daily Bread

THE FIRST CHURCH I SERVED, almost twenty years ago now, was in Orange City, Iowa. I was the associate pastor there and learned a lot about the basics of ministry: preaching, teaching, visitation, weddings, funerals, elder meetings, and staff meetings. It was a good place to start out. It was a big church in a small town in a mainly rural part of the country. It had doctors and lawyers and bank owners, but more than any other church I've ever been part of, or likely will ever be part of, it had lots of farmers. Generations of farmers, mostly growing corn and soybeans, with a few pigs here and there, and one very large dairy operation. I grew up with farmers in my extended family, but I was basically a child of the suburbs. So when I moved to Sioux County, Iowa, I had to learn about planting and harvest and seeds and combines and how much you could get for a bushel of corn.

Everyone, it seemed, knew stuff that I didn't know. They knew how to shingle a roof or finish a basement or change the oil in your car. People always knew which way was north, south, east, or west. They knew more about the weather and loved to talk about the weather, not just as small talk, but because the weather mattered a great deal in whether that year's harvest would be good or bad, great or awful. That corner of northwest Iowa is blessed with some of the best farmland in the world, and because the worst weather seems to hit South Dakota and Nebraska first, the farmers usually have very good harvests.

One of the things I'll never forget about pastoring there is the annual prayer service for crops and industry. That's exactly what it was called. Every year at the beginning of planting season, the church held a prayer service for the harvest that was six months away. From what I gathered, the prayer service had been around a long time. When I got there, the prayer service wasn't well attended. In fact, I wouldn't be surprised if the church has since discontinued the service. I could see when I was there that attendance was declining. Most of the attendees were old. There weren't as many farmers as there used to be in the community. And I imagine the prayer service didn't seem as urgent as it once did.

I don't tell the story to fault anyone for not having a prayer service for crops and industry. I doubt very many churches have ever had such a service. But there was something that really moved me about the tradition. It was not just a throwback to an earlier time in our history when most people lived on farms. It was a throwback to a less prosperous time in our history when many people's lives and livelihoods could be ruined if it didn't rain in May, or if a hailstorm came in June, or if a strange bug visited in July, or if the weather was unusually cold in August or September. That little prayer service was a way of reminding us that we actually, truly, undeniably need God. It's an easy lesson to forget when eating too much is a vastly more significant problem in America than not having enough to eat.

If there is one thing we can be certain God wants to teach us, surely it is to convince us once again that we are frail, life is fragile, and we depend upon God for everything. Think about that exhortation in James 4: "Come now, you who say, 'Today or tomorrow we will go into such and such a town and spend a year there and trade a make a profit.' . . . Instead you ought to say, 'If the Lord wills, we will live and do this or that'" (vv. 13, 15). As much as we may believe the myth of our self-sufficiency, the Lord's Prayer teaches us otherwise. Even in the land of plenty, we ought to pray day by day for our daily bread.

The Lord's Prayer consists of six petitions. The first three requests focus on *God's glory*—his name, his kingdom, and his will. The second set of three requests focuses on *our good*, and the first of these concerns is our provision of daily bread. Let's move step by step through each word of this petition.

Give

This first word in the petition, "Give," may sound too aggressive, like we are bossing God around, but remember that we are approaching our Father, and we are asking for what we need. I'm an imperfect father, but I'm never bothered by my children asking for what they truly need. And remember also that this isn't the first thing we pray. Jesus did not teach the disciples to begin their prayers with "Gimme." That's why the order matters; not that it needs to be followed in a robotic way, but getting the order right, at least in our hearts, prevents us from turning prayer into a

Christmas list of toys we want. Before we ask for ourselves, we are first concerned for God's name, God's kingdom, and God's will.

Coming from a humble heart, the word *give* is not just acceptable to God; it is pleasing to him. When we pray, God is not glad for demands, but he is glorified in our dependence. If my son says, "I expect a car on my sixteenth birthday," that is a demand that belittles me. But if he says, "I need your help because you know how to drive, and I don't," that expresses dependence that honors me. Never be afraid or embarrassed to cast all your cares on the Lord, for he cares for you (1 Pet. 5:7). More than that, the Lord Jesus repeatedly commands us to seek, knock, and ask (Matt. 7:7–11). Praying "give" is one way we honor the giver.

Us

The next word in the petition is "us." This quite literally is not a gimme prayer because the request is not "Give me" it is "Give us." As we see throughout the Lord's Prayer, it is presumed that we will be praying with others. We are together asking our Father for what we need. Even if we say this prayer individually, it is still important to pray the "us." Maybe your bread seems to be plentiful, but not everyone's cupboards are full. Not everyone has plenty of money in the bank. Not everyone has a house (or two) and two cars (or three or four). More than 10 percent of the American population live below the poverty line, and 10 percent of the world's population live on less than two dollars a day.

And, of course, as we will see, "bread" means more than just food. We are praying for the whole physical and spiritual well-being of God's people. And not just for their well-being, but their well-being for the sake of the first three petitions. "O, Lord, give us the sustenance and the life that we need that we may honor your name, that we may live for your kingdom, that we may obey your will."

This Day . . . Daily

Every word in this petition is important, but these may be the most important words for us: "this day" and the word that comes later, "daily." Jesus is teaching us a profound lesson in faith and dependence. We'd like to pray, "Father, give us in this moment and for every moment for the rest of our lives, everything we need." Boom, done. Finished. We've got a lifetime supply of bread lined up until heaven.

Several years ago at a fundraiser for school, we entered a raffle and got a call later that night that we had won a year's supply of Oodles of Noodles soup. When we learned of the prize, we thought we'd be swimming in pasta. I imagined a dump truck of pasta backing up to my house. But in reality we were given twelve coupons to use once a month for a year. That's not quite what I was thinking. We wanted all pasta, all the time. We didn't want a coupon book.

We would like to ask God to give us everything we need right now so we can see the supply of everything we need—a lifetime supply. But Jesus wants us to pray for what we need *this* day. He wants us to ask not for a lifetime supply of bread, but for our *daily* bread.[1]

This is the same lesson the Israelites had to learn on their way from Egypt to the promised land (Ex. 16). They wanted to collect enough manna for the week, but God gave them enough manna for the day (and enough for two days over the Sabbath). Of course, this doesn't mean we can't save money or that we have to live paycheck to paycheck. We see in both Testaments that material abundance can be a sign of God's favor and that investing and saving is prudent activity. Jesus isn't urging his disciples to start every day back at poverty. But he is commending to us a poverty of spirit. "Father in heaven, I'm not asking for your provision for six months from now. I'm asking that you give me what I need right now. Give me enough so that I can live the life you've called me to live *today*."

There's likely a connection in the Lord's prayer not only with Exodus 16 but with Proverbs 30. There the wise man asks the Lord for neither poverty nor riches, but to be fed "with the food that is needful for me" (30:8). The reason for that request is that we would not forget the Lord in our wealth or profane the name of the Lord by stealing in our poverty (v. 9). In other words, "Father, give us what we need for today so that we might hallow your name."

I said earlier that God wants us to grow in faith, which is why we are instructed to pray for this day's needs and not for the next thousand days. But the other thing God wants us to see is that we are more fragile than we think, and he is much kinder to us than we imagine. Even if your refrigerator is full of food and your retirement account looks good to go, you still must come to God each new day asking for bread. This isn't a mindless ritual. It's a confession that "normal" life can blow up anytime, that jobs and health and relationships and financial assets and national stability and global peace can be upended very quickly.

Years ago, when we had just moved to Michigan, a fire broke out in our home. The damage could have been a lot worse, but we had to stay out of the house for several months, and we had to make umpteen phone calls to clean and repair the house, and I had to spend numerous hours with the insurance company. It was massively inconvenient. Life can feel out of control so quickly. Our confidence for today is not that it will surely be like yesterday. Our confidence for today is that God is the same yesterday, today, and forever (Heb. 13:8). That's our only real security.

Our lives are much more fragile than we think. But here's the good news: God is much kinder to us than we imagine. Think about it: would you rather have God slop a year's worth of food in the trough or prepare you a meal every morning? God doesn't take care of us like my family would take care of our guinea pig. If we were going out of town for a few days, we figured we just needed to pour out three or four days of food for the guinea pig. "There you go, Fluffy, a big, huge mound of food. Don't eat it all at once. We'll see you on Monday." Is that all you want from your heavenly Father—just a big pile of treats so you can gorge yourself and not have to see him very often? That's not what we really need. And, thankfully, that's not what God gives us. He wants us to come every day so he can meet us every day so he can feed us every day.

Later in Matthew 6, Jesus talks about worry, which has everything to do with this prayer. There is a profound connection between "Give us this day our daily bread" and what Jesus has to say about worry at the end of Matthew 6. And let's be honest: all of us have occasions, sometimes moment by moment, where we are prone to worry.

You wake up ten minutes later than you had hoped and anxiety already starts to creep in: What if I'm late? What about traffic?

What's the weather like? You pass by the mirror and worry that your face has more wrinkles than it used to. You rush downstairs, and, because you are in a hurry, you let the kids eat whatever they want, so then you start to worry if sugar really does cause cancer. Maybe Lucky Charms is not a balanced diet. They are magically delicious, but maybe they're not magically nutritious. As you get the kids ready, you realize that one of your boys didn't do his homework—again. You worry about whether he's ever going to get his head screwed on straight, or if he'll get into college. As you drop the kids off, you worry that they may fall in with the wrong crowd or fall off the monkey bars. Once you get home, you pull up Facebook just to unwind. There you read about how awesome everyone else's kids are and all the amazing cupcakes your friends make, and you worry that you might be a failure as a mom.

Later in the morning, you want to go on a walk, but you feel that pain in your knee again. You worry about having to get knee-replacement surgery and whether your insurance will cover that, and how you'll pay for it, and who will take care of the kids if you are laid up for a month. Then you worry that maybe the pain is something worse, so you check all the medical websites and realize you probably have a rare case of whooping cough and African sleeping sickness.

Hours later, when the kids are in bed, you turn on the television to forget about the day. As you flip through the channels and get caught up on the news, you start to worry about the economy and cancel culture and declining morals. Then you see another shooting or another protest and worry about the racial divisions in this country and about how you'll talk to your friend who sees things a little differently. Maybe you worry about what the police would do to you. Maybe you worry about how people are going to treat your son who is a police officer. So, you turn off the television and talk to your husband and worry about his cough that doesn't seem to be getting better, as he tells you about the layoffs they're having at work.

Finally, as you lie down for the night, you feel a tremendous sense of anxiety, and you don't even know why. For reasons you can't understand, you start worrying about life and kids and your parents and your church and your health and flying and driving and sleeping and eating and a general fear that the days ahead could be really bad, and you can hardly sleep.

That's normal for many of us. But Jesus says it doesn't have to be that way. Three times he says do not be anxious (Matt. 6:25, 31, 34). And then he gives us all sorts of reasons why we shouldn't be anxious:

1. Life is too important (v. 25)
2. You are too important (v. 26)
3. It doesn't do any good (v. 27)
4. God cares about you (vv. 28–30)
5. Pagans worry (vv. 30–32)
6. The kingdom matters more (v. 33)
7. Tomorrow will be anxious for itself (v. 34)

Going through those seven points would take another chapter in itself, but just think about the last reason Jesus tells us not to worry: "Do not be anxious about tomorrow, for tomorrow will be anxious for itself" (v. 34). That's another way of saying, "Give us *this day* our daily bread."

Today's grace is for today's trials, and when tomorrow's trials come, God will have new grace waiting for you there. Sufficient for the day is its own trouble. Don't expect next year's bread today. Anxiety is living out the future before it gets here. You may look at other people and say, "I could never do what you're doing or endure what you've had to go through." You may see people who are martyrs for their faith or lose a job or lose their health or lose a loved one or become a widow or a widower and think, *I could never make it*. But of course you can't do that today; you don't have God's grace for tomorrow. Faith is trusting that when the future comes, our Father will be there to give us what we need. So Jesus is telling us not to be anxious about tomorrow. Don't start living out the troubles of next Tuesday because you haven't gotten to the grace that will be there waiting for you next Tuesday.

> The steadfast love of the LORD never ceases;
>> his mercies never come to an end;
> they are new every morning;
>> great is your faithfulness.
> "The LORD is my portion," says my soul,
>> "therefore I will hope in him." (Lam. 3:22–24)

Give us, not for all time, but this day our daily bread.

Our

I confess that for all the thousands of times I've said the Lord's Prayer I've never thought much about the word *our*—"Give us this day *our* daily bread" (Matt. 6:11). Many of the older commentaries rightly point out that *our* is a possessive word. We are not just asking that God give us any old bread, but that God would give us the bread that belongs to us.

At first blush, the request seems out of place. God doesn't owe us anything. How can we ask for *our* bread? By what reason do we have a right to claim it as ours? The Dutch theologian Herman Witsius (1636–1708) argued that when we say "our," we are taught industry and justice.[2] Industry, because praying for bread doesn't relieve us of the responsibility to work for that bread. We say "our" because in an earthly sense, we have earned what God is giving to us. And then justice, because *our* means we are not looking to take what does not belong to us. In other words, we do not expect to eat by sloth or by theft. We ask from God only what we need and what we could expect, given our steadfastness with the opportunities we have been given.

Bread

There is a long history in the church of interpreting "bread" both literally and spiritually. Augustine summarized the tradition of the early church when he argued that daily bread could refer to three things: (1) all things necessary for sustaining life, (2) the sacrament of the body of Christ, or (3) spiritual food.[3]

Certainly the first and most obvious meaning is physical bread, which includes more than just bread, but food in general. Mark 3:20 says, "Then he went home, and the crowd gathered again, so that they could not even eat." Translated woodenly it says, ". . . so that they were not able even to eat bread." Likewise, 2 Thessalonians 3:12 says, "Now such persons we command and encourage in the Lord Jesus Christ to do their work quietly and to earn their own living." In the Greek it says they must work quietly and "eat their own bread." Here again, we see the idea of *our* bread, meaning that which we have labored for. We also see that bread can mean any kind of food or really anything we truly need for living.

Notice that Jesus didn't direct the disciples to pray for specific national, international, or global concerns. Of course, it is good to pray for those things too. But it's worth noting that Jesus points us to rather mundane personal requests. We should not be embarrassed by these requests. We need food. We need water. We need clothing and shelter. God cares about the body and the soul.

We should not think that concerns for bodily sustenance and bodily pleasure are somehow beneath the Christian. True, we are not commanded to ask for our daily cake. Jesus is not encouraging a sense of entitlement or extravagance. And yet neither does he overlook the needs and nourishment of the body. The Bible never encourages asceticism as a way of life. God created marriage. God created food. It's the demons, not God, who forbid the enjoyment of these gifts (1 Tim. 4:3).

So "bread" is first of all real bread (and food and the necessities of life more broadly). But surely Jesus is also thinking of spiritual food. It is a repeated refrain in Scripture that man does not live by bread alone, but by every word that comes from the mouth of God (Deut. 8:3; Matt. 4:4). Praying for daily bread means asking God for *all* things necessary for life and godliness. Jesus would have us see that we can't live without bread, and we can't live without the Bible for very long either. "Don't just give us this earthly bread, but give us the bread that comes from the mouth of God."

Jesus is emphatic in his ministry that there is better bread out there, that we should seek the heavenly bread that can feed us not just for a day but for all eternity. Most importantly, Jesus makes clear that *he* is the bread of life (John 6:35). He is the bread come down from heaven (6:41), and whoever feasts on him will live forever (6:54). When we pray the Lord's Prayer and come to this petition day after day, our hearts should be singing that great simple song "Give Me Jesus."[4]

Three Last Things

Isn't it amazing how much there is to learn and think about in the simple and familiar requests of the Lord's Prayer? "Give us bread" sounds pretty straightforward, until we realize God wants to fill our hearts even more than he wants to fill our stomachs. Let me give you three words in closing that get to the heart of what Jesus wants in our hearts. This fourth petition teaches us a spirit of contentment, a spirit of gratitude, and a spirit of dependence.

A Spirit of Contentment

Richard Coekin, in his book on the Lord's Prayer, tells the story of a wealthy and generous Christian businessman he knows who lost a fortune in the Enron scandal. Reflecting on where he had worked and all that he had lost, through no fault of his own, the man remarked, "I have repeatedly acknowledged to God that my wealth comes from him. I've asked that, if at any point he thought it would be spiritually better for me not to have it, he would please take it away. I trust that this is what he has done and I am content with that."[5] Asking for daily bread reminds us that godliness with contentment is great gain (1 Tim. 6:6).

A Spirit of Gratitude

James 1:17 says, "Every good and perfect gift is from above, coming down from the Father of lights, with whom there is no variation or shadow due to change." Not just some good gifts, but *every* good gift. Do you have kids? A spouse? Friends? A job? A good church? A new sweater? A favorite ice cream to eat? A favorite song to sing? A book to read? Do you have shoes, socks, and underwear? Do you have a bed to sleep on? Do you laugh? Do you have money in the bank? Do you have a Bible to read? Every good gift has come down from the Father of lights. Give thanks to God. If you are a Christian you can be sure that God has taken care of you in the past, he knows your needs in the present, and he has prepared for you a lavish feast to come. "Rejoice in the Lord always; again I say, rejoice" (Phil. 4:4).

Dependence

I imagine most of us thank God for our daily bread every day. We pray around the dinner table and thank him for our food. That's good. But how often do we ask him for our food? For most of us, we don't ask for it because we assume it. We expect not just daily bread but cupboards and stores full of bread. In one sense, this is a tremendous blessing. But it's also a profound danger. More than almost any people who have ever lived, we are tempted to forget God. Praying this prayer reminds us of our dependence upon him.

The word *daily* suggests that we are to pray this prayer, or something like it, every day. "Dear Father, today I need your help. Today I need your blessing. Today I need your provision." Come to God with your requests. Honor him by trusting in his goodness and depending on his power. When Jesus fed the five thousand, he wasn't just performing a miracle to show that he was divine. He was teaching them the invaluable lesson that he is more than able to take care of all their needs.

Look to God to satisfy you (Ps. 145:15–16). Seek his blessing each morning. "Unless the LORD builds the house, those who build it labor in vain. Unless the LORD watches over the city, the watchman stays awake in vain" (Ps. 127:1–2). I love what the Heidelberg Catechism says: "Neither our work and worry nor your gifts can do us any good without your blessing" (Question and Answer 125). It's only in the Lord that our labors are not in vain (1 Cor. 15:58).

We do not glorify God by trying to do things on our own so as not to bother him. Don't think, "You're a very busy God; you've got a lot going on; you probably have many more important things to deal with in the world." The great thing about God is that he's God. He's the only one who can truly multitask.

He can receive all of our requests. You don't honor him by trying to do it on your own and then suggesting, "I'll see you in ten years if something really bad happens." We glorify God by coming to him each day for daily bread.

I need thee ev'ry hour,
In joy or pain;
Come quickly and abide,
Or life is vain.
I need thee, O I need thee;
Ev'ry hour I need thee!
O, bless me now, my Savior!
I come to thee.[6]

5

Our Debts

I REMEMBER HEARING A PASTOR say years ago that you could give the secret to a good marriage in just one word. The word he gave was not *money* or *sex* or *communication* or even *love*. The word was *forgive*. Forgiveness is the key ingredient not only in marriage but in any relationship involving sinners. If your friends are going to stick around, if you are going to see your relatives more than once a year, if you plan to work in the same place with the same people for any length of time, if you want to be happy in the church (or simply not give up on the church), you need to learn forgiveness. You need to grant it, and you need to receive it.

What's true in our horizontal relationships is also true in our vertical relationship. Of course, God is not a sinner. He never needs to be forgiven. But if we are to have a healthy relationship with our heavenly Father, we must often come before him confessing our sins and asking for grace.

We can look at this fifth petition in those two categories: our vertical relationship with God and our horizontal relationships with others. We can label these two realities the forgiveness we need to receive and the forgiveness we need to give.

The Forgiveness We Need to Receive

We need daily bread that we might live and daily forgiveness that we might not die. If we ask every day for bread, it stands to reason that we also ask God every day for grace for our debts. We owe to God what we cannot pay. That makes us debtors.

Does it matter if we say "debts and debtors" or "trespasses and those who trespass against us"? We need an international council to settle this and make corporate prayer much easier! It doesn't matter a lot, but it may matter a little. Matthew 6:12 has the word *debts*, Matthew 6:14 has *trespasses*, and Luke 11:4 has *sins*—three different English words for three different Greek words. So whether we pray for our debts our trespasses or our sins to be forgiven, we pray biblically. The words mean roughly the same thing.

But they don't mean exactly the same thing. The word *trespass* suggests that we have violated a rule or committed an infraction. The word *debt* suggests we owe God something we cannot pay. "Forgive us our debts" suggests that we have done things that we should not have done, and left undone things we should have done.

"Forgive us our trespasses" comes from the Book of Common Prayer, which is why many people use the word *trespasses*. The Geneva Bible and the King James Bible used the word *debts*. If you know your church history, you know that the Book of Common Prayer was and is still used by the Anglican Church. So denominations that came out of the Church of England—Episcopal,

Wesleyan, Methodist—tend to use *trespasses*, while most everyone else says *debts*.

The only other place the Greek word *opheilema* (debt) occurs in the New Testament is in Romans 4:4, where it clearly refers to a debt, or what someone is owed. Likewise, the word *opheiletes* is consistently employed to mean "debtor" in the rest of the New Testament (Matt. 18:24; Luke 13:4; Rom. 1:14; 4:4; 8:12; 15:27; Gal. 5:3). Every English translation I can find, except for the loosely translated New Living Translation, uses "debts" in Matthew's version of the Lord's Prayer.

More important, however, than getting the word right is getting the idea right. Every day, we live as debtors to mercy. Do you believe that? Do you believe that just as you have needs to ask for every day, so you have sins that need to be forgiven every day? And notice the word in the prayer is not *debt* but *debts*, as in many. Every single debt deserves to be met with God's righteous displeasure, but think about the many debts we owe to God, debts that we are powerless to pay. Herman Witsius makes this point powerfully:

> Had we contracted by one debt of this kind, would not the thought of it have been enough to fill our mind with indescribable horror? But we are chargeable with *debts*—debts of every description: original, imputed, inherent; [and] actual, debts of omission and commission, of ignorance, infirmity, and deliberate wickedness, without limits and without number.[1]

At this point, some Christians may ask, "Why, if we have already been redeemed, cleansed, and justified, do we need to keep asking for forgiveness?" I remember well at my church a godly woman who objected to our weekly confession of sin. She thought it was a real downer and encouraged wallowing in our sins when God wanted us to know we were forgiven and free. She believed it was wrong for justified sinners to return to their sins over and over.

So why does Jesus teach us to pray, "Forgive us our debts," and not just once but frequently, if not daily? Well, for starters, we still sin. We ask for forgiveness for our debts because we never stop being debtors. But more than that, it's because Jesus wants us to relate to God not just as a judge but as a father. This is such an important point and one that sincere Christians often miss. If you think of God only as judge, then you are either innocent or guilty. You are justified or not justified. You don't think in terms of pleasing or displeasing God. You think only in terms of the legal declaration of righteous or not righteous. As important as it is to recognize that God is judge, if that's the only way you relate to him, your Christianity will become stilted and stale.

God is also our Father, and that's explicitly how Jesus wants us to address him in the Lord's Prayer. A good father always loves his children, but he can be pleased or displeased with them. You wouldn't go back to the judge to admit another mistake, but you would go to your father to say you're sorry. When my kids do what they shouldn't do or fail to do what I asked of them, I don't want them fearing that they are going to be disowned and booted out of the family. But neither do I want them to think that their disobedience is no big deal. If they are good children—and if they know I am a good father—they will come to me and acknowledge their sins, and I will be eager to forgive them.

So if I sin as a Christian, I should not fear condemnation, for there is no condemnation for those who are in Christ Jesus, but I should still feel pricked in my conscience. I should not despair, but I should feel guilty when I do things that deserve to be punished. I have disrupted the Father-son relationship I enjoy with God. That's why I should ask for forgiveness—not to be justified all over again, but because I have made a mess of the most important relationship in my life. The prayer "Forgive us our debts" is the cry not of a frightened litigant but of a loving child.

The Forgiveness We Need to Give

There is a second half to this petition: "Forgive us our debts, *as we also have forgiven our debtors* (Matt. 6:12). In this fifth petition, we not only ask something of God; we also expect something of ourselves. Forgiven people forgive. It's as simple as that. If you never forgive, you ought to wonder if you have ever truly experienced and really believed in forgiveness.

At this point, it may be helpful to be more specific as to what we mean by *forgiveness* because there is a lot of confusion generated by misunderstanding what exactly forgiveness is and isn't. How would you define forgiveness by simply looking at verse 12? Forgiveness is something like canceling a debt or remitting a payment. That's the basic idea. When God forgives us, he says, "I will not make you pay me what you owe me." When we forgive others, we say something similar: "I will not demand of you the moral payment that is rightfully mine." We understand that it is not our place to pass final judgment on another person's sins, because every sin that has ever been committed has either been punished on the cross or will be punished in hell.

We need to be clear, however, what forgiveness is not.

1. Forgiveness is not the absence of consequences. A dad may forgive his son for staying out late, but he may be grounded for his disobedience. The son may experience discipline just like we may experience discipline from God, even when there is forgiveness.

2. Forgiveness does not eliminate all authority structures. There are consequences for violating parental authority. Likewise, there are consequences for violating governmental authority. You may be personally forgiven for a wrong done but may face prison or even a death sentence. The thief on the cross was not removed from the cross just because he confessed his sins. Similarly, there are consequences for violating ecclesiastical authority (Matt. 18; 1 Cor. 5). When a sinner goes on sinning without repentance, the church is obligated to act and discipline. The church must never be judgmental, but it is explicitly the church's duty to judge (1 Cor. 5:12).

3. Forgiveness is not the complete absence of any judgment. There is a right way and a wrong way to judge. We see this in Matthew 7. Do not judge, Jesus says, but then he goes on to teach that his disciples aren't to cast their pearls before swine (7:6), which requires making a judgment as to who the swine are. The kind of judging we are to avoid sees only the negative, believes only what is critical, and always assumes the worst about other's motives. That's judgmental*ism*. That's not the same as making a wise evaluation. A charitable judgment of others does not require us to be unthinking, unquestioning, and undiscerning. We are to be wise as serpents and innocent as doves (Matt. 10:16). When Jesus tells us to forgive, he does not mean we are to play with rattlesnakes as if they're puppies. Forgiveness means that if the

rattlesnake becomes a puppy, we won't always remind him that he used to be a snake.

A Definition Please

So what is forgiveness? Zacharias Ursinus, in his commentary on the Heidelberg Catechism, explains forgiveness in a helpful way. Forgiveness, he says, can take three different forms, and only one must always be present. Forgiveness is threefold:

1. *Of revenge.* This pertains to all. When we forgive we won't seek revenge.
2. *Of punishment.* This will not always be removed. For God desires that his law be executed.
3. *Of judgment* in reference to others. "This should not always be remitted; for God who prohibits falsehood, will not have us to judge of knaves as honest men, but he designs that we should distinguish the good from the bad."[2]

In other words, forgiving is not always the same as forgetting. Often when we talk about forgiving those who sin against us, we have in mind our own internal state. But the older, and I would say more biblical, view of forgiveness is that forgiveness is a relational transaction more than a therapeutic one. Forgiveness is an act of the will. According to the Puritan Thomas Watson, forgiveness means "we strive against all thoughts of revenge; when we will not do our enemies mischief, but wish well to them, grieve at their calamities, pray for them, seek reconciliation with them and show ourselves ready on all occasions to relieve them."[3] I hate to say it, but Inigo Montoya was not really modeling Christian virtue when he devoted his whole life to avenging his father's death.

Many Christians, influenced by well-meaning but misguided counseling and a lot of pop psychology, have a therapeutic understanding of forgiveness. They think of forgiveness as a unilateral, internal effort to get our emotions under control. But if we start with a biblical notion of God's forgiveness, we see that such a view falls short. This is the point Chris Brauns makes in his important book *Unpacking Forgiveness*.[4] Several years ago I interviewed Chris on my blog, and I asked him about our culture's therapeutic notion of forgiveness. What he said then is worth repeating:

> Therapeutic forgiveness insists that forgiveness is at its core a feeling. Our culture has picked up on this in a big way. When most people say that they forgive, they mean that it is a private matter in which he or she is not going to feel bitter.
>
> Borrowing a line from Boston's *Don't Look Back* album, I argue that forgiveness is "More Than a Feeling." Biblical forgiveness is something that happens between two parties. When God forgives us, our relationship with him is restored. That is why Calvin said that the whole of the Gospel is contained under the headings of repentance and forgiveness of sins (*Institutes* 3.3.19).
>
> Once people make forgiveness therapeutic, you have all sorts of nonbiblical things happening. For instance, some say it is legitimate to forgive God. This is a heretical idea because God has never done anything which requires forgiveness. But "therapeutic" forgiveness needs to forgive God so bitterness is no longer felt.

Therapeutic forgiveness also diminishes the necessity of two parties working out their differences. If forgiveness is simply how I feel, there is no need to worry about the relationship.

The tragedy of therapeutic forgiveness is that in making individual feelings the center of everything, I think it ultimately leads to bitterness and the wrong feelings.[5]

Overcoming anger and resentment is important, but forgiveness is something more, something different, something that involves two parties instead of one. Forgiveness is what we grant to people when they repent. While we should always have an attitude of forgiveness and put forward a sincere offer of forgiveness, the fullest expression of biblical forgiveness happens when one side repents and the other side removes the moral debt he is owed.

I think of the scene in the movie *Braveheart* where William Wallace kneels before his father-in-law after his daughter was killed because she was Wallace's wife. The father struggles for a moment but then puts his hand on the head of William Wallace, indicating that he will forgive him though his daughter would not have died if she had not secretly married Wallace.[6] That's forgiveness. "You are no longer in my debt. You do not owe me anything. I will not hold anything over your head. You do not have to work something off for me to accept you. What you should give me to make up for my loss I no longer ask of you."

Forgiven and Forgiving

We return here to the fifth petition in the Lord's Prayer.

I needed to go through the definition of *forgiveness* carefully so that you can feel the proper weight of the fifth petition. The

Bible is clear that the *unforgiving* person is an *unforgiven* person. Are we saved by our forgiving heart? No, of course not. Our forgiving heart does not merit God's forgiveness. But a forgiving heart is a condition for God's forgiveness. It doesn't matter what experience you think you had or what prayer you prayed; if you don't forgive, you won't be forgiven.

Amazingly, we are asking God, in a manner of speaking, to follow our example. "God, please treat me as I treat other people." That's a bold request, and it really makes us consider whether we would want God doing to us as we do to others. We should not understand the connection in Matthew 6:12 to be a legalistic formula: "God, I scratched their back, so you scratch mine." It's not a statement of manipulation. It's a statement of recognition. Only the one who forgives can expect to be forgiven. Or, to state the same thing in the other direction, the one who knows that his sins have been forgiven by God will, in turn, be eager to forgive those who sin against him.

Forgiveness is one of the most overlooked aspects of Christian discipleship. Think of what Jesus says earlier in the Sermon on the Mount. If someone legitimately has something against you, leave the worship service right on the spot and go take care of that relationship. In other words, even prayer should be interrupted so that forgiveness can be sought (Matt. 5:23–24). Think about all the places in the New Testament that stress the importance of our attitude toward others and our forgiveness of others.

> With the judgment you pronounce you will be judged, and with the measure you use it will be measured to you. (Matt. 7:2)

Then his master summoned him and said to him, "You wicked servant! I forgave you all that debt because you pleaded with me. And should not you have had mercy on your fellow servant, as I had mercy on you?" (Matt. 18:32–33)

Be kind to one another, tenderhearted, forgiving one another, as God in Christ forgave you. (Eph. 4:32)

There is nothing as important in your life as asking God to forgive you your debts, and maybe nothing as hard as God asking you to forgive your debtors.

Conclusion

Let me finish this chapter with two questions.

First, are you keeping from God all that you should place at his feet? Perhaps your relationship with God is ruptured because you have not confessed your sins. Have you become blind to your sins because you never think to include this fifth petition in your prayers? Are you avoiding an honest admission of what you've really been doing? Nothing can be kept hidden in his sight. Don't you want to know the joy of a clean conscience and restored relationship with your heavenly Father?

Second, are you demanding of others what God has not demanded of you? Listen again to Witsius: "When God forgives, he frees the sinner from everlasting punishment, and blesses him with his favour, which is the fountain of life and of all happiness. But when we forgive, we merely cease to indulge towards the offender our feeble, and perhaps impotent wrath, and bestow upon him our best wishes."[7] God's forgiveness is so much grander than ours. Do not ask your neighbor, your spouse, your parent, or your friend to pick up the tip when someone else has already bought you the whole meal. What would it look like if God treated you and your sins in the same way you treated those who sin against you? No doubt, some people have hurt you deeply. God never says it's no big deal what happened to you. Forgiveness is not saying that sin doesn't matter. You're not saying it's no big deal. You're saying God is bigger, the cross is bigger, and hell is bigger. Do not focus on what they owe. Focus on what God has already forgiven you.

6

Our Plea

I'VE ENJOYED RUNNING FOR YEARS and have been a fairly consistent (though not spectacular) runner ever since middle school. Over decades of running, I can think of several times when I realized, almost too late, that I was in somewhat serious danger.

A few years ago, I was running on a dirt road, winding through the hilly terrain of western North Carolina when I saw a pit bull coming toward me. It left the front yard it was sitting in and started fast-walking in my direction with a low growl. I stopped running and calmly started walking in the opposite direction. The dog wasn't running, so I kept walking. He followed me quite a way from his home, while his owners didn't seem the least bit concerned either that their dog was gone or that he was stalking an innocent stranger. Eventually the dog must have figured I was safely away from his domain. He broke off his trot, turned around, and went back home, and I lived to tell the tale.

Another time I was running in a beautiful section of woods that lies between Gordon-Conwell Theological Seminary and Gordon

College. It was a crisp, sunny, beautiful, late-fall afternoon in New England. It was such an idyllic setting that I jogged off the trail and was scampering among the trees. At that time of the year in New England, the sun starts setting at 4:30. Before I knew it, it was getting dark, and I realized I had no idea where I was. This was before the days of GPS watches or smartphones or running lights. I started to panic a little and to think about how cold it would be sleeping under a pile of leaves. I decided to run as fast as I could in whatever direction seemed most downhill, hoping that would lead to a road or a stream or something. Eventually, I did hit a gravel road and was able to follow that back to something familiar, but I was about 10 minutes away from needing a troop of brave wilderness explorers to come and rescue me in the woods.

One last story, and this was probably the scariest, though I didn't know it at the time. I was living in Colorado for the summer. I was staying in a beautiful but very backwoods rustic location. I was running on a dirt road one day when I decided to head off the path (see a theme?) and run up into the hills. As I was making my way along the ridge I came across a large deer or elk that was lying dead on the ground. It wasn't decaying or torn apart, so the animal must not have been dead very long. I thought to myself, *Whatever killed this large, fast animal is going to have a very easy time killing me.* Later people told me I was probably very close to being in big trouble from a black bear.

Thankfully, in all three circumstances I realized I was in danger before it was too late. But only barely (no pun intended!). What's true with running in the wilderness areas off the beaten path is even more true in our spiritual lives. We seldom realize the danger we are in and sometimes not until it *is* too late. The last thing Jesus wants to teach us in the Lord's Prayer is that we need our Father's help because we are full of danger within us and stalked by danger around us.

An Order of Importance

We come now to the sixth petition, "Lead us not into temptation, but deliver us from evil" (Matt. 6:13). Some people divide this into two petitions, but we will see that these two requests are really the same request expressed in two parallel halves.

This is not only the sixth petition overall, but the third and final petition in this second set of three requests focused on our good. You can almost see a Trinitarian structure in the prayer. God the Father is the Creator and provider who gives us our daily bread. God the Son is the atonement for our sins. And God the Spirit leads us and fills us with power to live a holy life. When we know our sins have been covered, it doesn't lead us to be cavalier with sin and darkness. "But with you there is forgiveness that you may be feared" (Ps. 130:4). Once set free, we want to walk in the light as he is in the light (1 John 1:7).

The Lord's Prayer, in addition to teaching us how to pray, teaches us about ourselves. These last three requests give voice to the three things every human being needs: provision, pardon, and protection. We have stomachs to be filled, sins to be forgiven, and evil to be fought. If you want one more alliterative triad, these three petitions remind us that we live a life of dependence, debts, and danger.

Tempted and Tried

The request seems simple enough—"Lead us not into temptation"—until we try to define what *temptation* is. There are at least three different kinds of temptations in the Bible.

1. Sometimes the Bible portrays *temptations as trials or testing.* These trials are not in themselves sinful, but the suffering they entail can tempt us to doubt God, or compromise with the world, or give up on the faith. James 1:2 says, "Count it all joy, my brothers, when you meet trials of various kinds." The Greek word translated "trials" is *peirasmois.* It's the same word used in verb form in James 1:13 that is translated several times as "tempted" or "tempts." So *temptation* can refer broadly to the suffering, tribulation, and trials that we are called to endure.

2. Sometimes the Bible thinks of *temptations as enticement to sin.* These temptations can arise from without, external to us. Think of Jesus's temptations in the wilderness. He had no sin nature lusting after what was wrong. Yes, Jesus was tempted in every way as we are (yet without sin). He was a true human, and yet that doesn't mean that his *experience* of temptation was in every way identical to our experience. He was tempted externally by the devil's entreaties and suggestions. Likewise, we can also be tempted from the outside by the world's lies and promises.

3. Then there are those *temptations that arise from within*, those allurements to sin that are internal, originating from the power of indwelling sin. This is what James means when he says, "Each person is tempted when he is lured and enticed by his own desire" (James 1:14). These are the temptations Christ did not experience. He had no sinful lusts. He had no misplaced desires in his heart. Jesus was tempted in suffering by trials and by the devil's words but not from within by fallen desires. We are tempted by all three; Jesus was tempted by the first two.

What does it mean, then, to pray, "Lead us not into temptation"? It doesn't mean, "Do not entice me to sin." God never entices us to sin. James 1:13 says, "Let no one say when he is tempted, 'I am being tempted by God,' for God cannot be tempted with evil, and he himself tempts no one." "The LORD tests the righteous" (Ps. 11:5), but he does not tempt us; that is, he does not present before us sin as an attraction. It would be inconsistent with God's character for him ever to present sin to us in order to entice us.

Notice, the Lord's Prayer does not say, "Father, do not tempt me." That is a wholly unnecessary prayer. Rather it says, "Do not *lead* me into temptation." That means, "Do not allow me to be near the allure of sin. Do not bring me near to the devil. Do not permit me to be in a situation where the enticement to sin will be greater than I can bear." That's what Jesus is teaching us to pray.

If we look at the context in Matthew's Gospel, we can see the meaning more clearly in the Lord's Prayer: "Then Jesus was led up by the Spirit into the wilderness to be tempted by the devil" (Matt. 4:1). Jesus had a special mission to fulfill. He had to succeed where the first Adam failed. He had to prove faithful in the wilderness when Israel had proved faithless. The Spirit led Jesus into the place of testing and temptation. Jesus teaches us to pray, "Father, do not lead me into that same haunted wilderness."

This doesn't mean that God will never providentially arrange for trials in our life; surely he does. We see in Job how he allowed Job to be tested. We do not pray for a life set apart from all suffering. We pray for a life set apart from sinning. This is why we should read "lead us not . . ." in conjunction with ". . . deliver us from." Typical Hebrew parallelism says one thing and then says the same thing with different language. So "lead us not into temptation" is a poetic way of expressing the same thing as the second half of the verse, "deliver us from evil." At its most basic level, this sixth petition is a request for spiritual protection.

That's why I think "evil" at the end of the verse probably has in mind "the evil one." The Greek is *tou ponerou*, which can be a neuter noun meaning "evil" or a masculine noun meaning "the evil one." Given the connection with Jesus's temptation in the wilderness, I think the noun is likely in the masculine form and should be taken as a reference to the devil. We are praying to God, "Keep me out of the path of sin, and keep me safe from the devil's snares."

Think of all the things we are expressing to God when we make this simple request. We are making known our hatred for sin and confessing our weakness to overcome it. We are counting on God to never leave us or forsake us. We are trusting in the power of the Spirit to be our strength and our shield. Jesus does not instruct us to pray for more willpower to do the right thing, even if our wills must always be engaged in the fight against sin. Our prayer is not for the courage to fight but for our heavenly Father to be our refuge, our rock, and our rescue.

Once again, remember that we are praying to our heavenly Father. He is not too busy to care, and he is not too impotent to help. I think of the times my young kids have said, "Dad, don't let my head go underwater." "Dad, don't leave me in the store by myself." "Dad, you'll sit next to me on the plane, right?" I love requests like that. They honor me as a father. They are not hard for me. And it brings me delight to guide and to guard my children. How much more does your heavenly Father love to guide and to guard you?

Jesus's Temptations and Ours

As we think about temptation in our life, it's helpful to think about the temptation Jesus faced, because the sort of things that the devil presented to Jesus are the same things that he will present to us. The devil tempted Jesus in the wilderness with pleasure, pride, and power.

Pleasure

You can see what the devil is up to: "You're hungry Jesus. You've been fasting for forty days and nights. Have a bite to eat. You're the Son of God, aren't you? Then give yourself what you want. It's just bread. Go ahead and eat. Turn these stones into loaves."

Not all pleasure is sinful, just like not all eating is wrong. Matthew 4:11 says that the angels came and ministered to him, which probably means they brought him food, just like the angel of the Lord brought food to Elijah in the wilderness in 1 Kings 19. Eating per se was not the problem. The question was whether Jesus would listen to the devil. Would Jesus try to prove his identity on the devil's terms? Did Jesus love God more than food? Did Jesus trust that God could satisfy his hunger another way?

Jesus fought pleasure with pleasure. "Man shall not live by bread alone, but man lives by every word that comes from the mouth of the Lord" (Deut. 8:3). In other words, "I don't need your food, Satan, in order to be full. God sustains me. God is with me."

> A day in your courts is better
>> than a thousand elsewhere. (Ps. 84:10)

Your steadfast love is better than life. . . .
My soul will be satisfied as with fat and rich food.
(Ps. 63:3, 5)

Whom have I in heaven but you?
And there is nothing on earth I desire besides you.
My flesh and my heart may fail,
but God is the strength of my heart and my portion
forever. (Ps. 73:25–26)

Jesus fought pleasure with pleasure. You're presenting to me the immediate pleasure of bread, but I have from my heavenly Father greater pleasure in his word.

Pride

The second temptation is for Jesus to prove himself: "Come on Jesus, show what you can do. Put on a big show. Jump off the temple and command the angels to be your parachute. You'll be famous. Everyone will be talking about you. This will be the most amazing thing these people ever see. They'll have no doubt that you are the Son of God."

Satan even quotes Scripture (Ps. 91:11–12). But he does not apply it correctly. People can bring you Scripture, but that doesn't mean that they're telling you the truth. The devil turns a text of promise into an opportunity for pride. It certainly wouldn't have been wrong for people to see Jesus's power. It wasn't wrong for the disciples to worship him after the resurrection. There's nothing wrong with Jesus revealing his glory, but this was not the way to do it. God is not a carnival attraction.

God does not exist to do tricks for us. God wants heartfelt worship, not mere fame.

Jesus's response, in Matthew 4:7, is to quote Deuteronomy 6:16: "You shall not put the Lord your God to the test." Do not put God on trial. Do not back God into a corner. Do not insist that God fill out your final exam. He does not need to prove himself to us, and he does not exist to make us look good to others.

Power

In the final temptation, the devil proposes a shortcut to glory. "Look at all the kingdoms of the world. Just worship me and it will all be yours." What the devil offered was not wrong. Jesus will later say, "All authority in heaven and on earth has been given to me" (Matt. 28:18). All the kingdoms would be his. But the devil proposes the right end through the wrong means. The devil wants us to take shortcuts. He says, "Look, Jesus, all the kingdoms—they can be yours. No suffering. No betrayal. No cross. You can get where you want to go much more easily, much more comfortably, by doing it my way. It doesn't have to be so hard, Jesus. You can have the whole world. You have all the power and glory you want. Just fall at my feet."

The temptation was to power. It was also a temptation to shortcuts. Satan always tempts us with the easy way out. He always offers a crown without the cross, pleasure without the pain, success without the sacrifice, admiration without affliction. He promises to give us everything God can give us but, unlike God, he'll get us to the top of the mountain without our having to walk through the valley.

Jesus saw through the devil's counterfeit currency: "You shall worship the Lord your God, and him only shall you serve" (Matt.

4:10, citing Deut. 6:13). Jesus understood that God's end must always be accomplished by God's means. The devil lures us with legitimate things, like influence and purpose, and tempts us to get them by illegitimate means. Sometimes he gets us to go after the wrong things. Other times he gets us to go after the right things in the wrong way or for the wrong reasons. He is a deceiver. He excels in presenting half-truths. He masquerades as an angel of light. He promises what he cannot deliver.

You could make a good case that these three temptations—pleasure, pride, and power—have been the same tricks of the devil since the very beginning. "So when the woman saw that the tree was good for food, and that it was a delight to the eyes, and that the tree was to be desired to make one wise, she took of its fruit and ate, and she also gave some to her husband who was with her, and he ate" (Gen. 3:6). Adam and Eve wanted God's blessings on their own terms. They wanted what looked beautiful. They wanted the right to decide for themselves good from evil. They wanted the influence that comes from wisdom. They wanted pleasure, pride, and power.

We hear echoes of the same triad in 1 John 2:16: "All that is in the world—the desires of the flesh and the desires of the eyes and pride in possessions—is not from the Father but is from the world." The world promises you everything. The world dangles the bait and hides the hook. The world says, "Love me, not God. Love me, and your flesh will be satisfied. Love me, and your eyes will have whatever they want. Love me, and you can be rich and famous." The world promises pleasure, pride, and power. But it never lasts.

You can be sure that when the devil tempts you, he will come with the same three things. Where is your weakness? You could be decked out in the best armor, but if you have one open spot of weakness, the rest of the armor won't do you any good.

Some people don't care about being famous. They aren't interested in being in control. But they want to feel good. They will sacrifice everything for ease and comfort. They want pleasure. That's where the devil will come at them.

Other people want recognition. They are willing to work hard for it. They can be disciplined and forgo creature comforts. They don't even care about being in control. They want to be famous. They want people talking about them. They want to nurture their pride. They want "likes" and "follows" and people to pat them on the back and think they're amazing.

And there are those who aren't interested in what people think about them. They may even fancy themselves sort of above all that. They aren't trying to be liked or impressive. They aren't trying to go at things the easy way. But they want to be in the inner circle. They don't care if they eat, sleep, and drink. They just want to make it to the top. They want to be in the know. They want to be in control. They want to have authority. They want to be calling the shots. They want power.

Where are you most likely to be tempted? We're all different. You may look at the temptation that someone else struggles with and think, "Why would you even care about having that?" and fancy yourself to be immune from temptation, when actually there's some other area of sin that your friend is not drawn to while you are daydreaming about it all the time.

Or if we can ask the question with a different metaphor, in which room is the devil most likely to whisper into your ear? Is it the bedroom with its pleasures, the boardroom with its power, or the bathroom mirror with its pride? Know your enemy. Know yourself. And know from whence your help comes.

Dangerous Journey

Perhaps more than anything else, this last petition reminds us that we live perilous lives—danger within and danger without. We all know too well—we have stories to tell—of people who seemed to be very strong, seemed to be walking with the Lord, when they gave into temptation in tragic ways. I think of a young man I knew who seemed to be on fire for the Lord and earnest in his faith. His father had walked out on their family when the young man was a boy, and he was determined not to do the same thing. But some years later, he did exactly the same thing, though calling himself a Christian and convincing himself that there was a reason to walk out and leave his wife and kids and go on to something better. He had believed lies about himself, about where happiness comes from, and about what God is like and wants.

Do not be caught unaware. "Whoever has God for his friend," Witsius wrote, "will find Satan to be his enemy."[1] You can count on it. The road we have to travel is narrow, and the enemies on the path are fierce and cunning. Most of us, if we're honest, live our lives too serious about casual things and too casual about serious things. We fret about clothes and calories. We fuss about diets and home decor. Our whole week can be ruined by a sporting event gone wrong. We are supremely concerned about these relatively unimportant matters. And yet we will start each new day as if we were in no spiritual danger, as if we had no enemy, as if we were not at war with our flesh.

We know that we need daily bread. We may even know that we need forgiveness. But do we know how much we need this prayer each day? If we are to pray for daily provision and daily pardon, then we must also pray for daily protection. How many times do we go about each day thinking that there is no battle, blissfully ignorant, sometimes willfully ignorant, of the danger that we will face?

When I think of this petition, I always think of the story of Potiphar's wife. Joseph didn't know when he got up that morning the temptation he would face. He had faced it before, but never so brazenly. He didn't know that he would be seduced in secret by a beautiful and powerful woman. But he was. And when he was, he was ready. He did not ponder the temptation. He did not nurture it. He did not reason with it. He made a much better decision. He ran away from it. Are you getting spiritually prepared in prayer each morning for the possibility of a Potiphar's wife, in whatever form that may take in your life? Are you pleading with God, "Do not present to me such temptation, do not lead me in the path where such allurements can come my way"? Will you be ready? Are you praying for that protection?

You probably know that on Sunday morning, December 7, 1941, the Japanese military launched a surprise attack on the US naval fleet stationed at Pearl Harbor. The Americans were not as prepared as they should have been, even though there were signs of imminent danger. A Gallup poll taken just before the Pearl Harbor attack showed that 52 percent of Americans expected war with Japan, and only 27 percent did not. The American public was expecting something. Everyone knew something was coming. On December 6, US intelligence intercepted a Japanese message asking about ship movements and the location of naval vessels at Pearl Harbor. A cryptologist gave the message to her supervisor, who said he would look at it after the weekend and get back to her on Monday. Early on the morning of December 7 a radar operator on Oahu spotted a large group of airplanes heading for the island. He told his supervisor, who said it must be American B-17 bombers on a training run. The danger was there. People saw the signs. But they were not ready.

There is no way to fully escape sin in this life. You could be like the monks of old and live your life on top of a column or in a cave somewhere, and you would still have the devil attacking you, and you would have your flesh to battle. We cannot avoid suffering. We will not avoid human trials. But we can pray for divine deliverance. Do you know that you need help? And do you know that there is help? He who is in you is greater than he who is in the world (1 John 4:4). Resist the devil and he will flee from you (James 4:7). Mark it very well: we carry within us by the Spirit the power to withstand the evil one, and we have his word outside of us and working within us to enable us to overcome the darkness. There is power available for you right now. Will you go about this day and this week knowing that there is a battle? We know we are in spiritual danger. But we must also never forget that we have a heavenly Father who would love to give us all the protection we need, all the air cover we need, to guide us and to guard us and to protect us if we would pray.

7

His Glory

IF YOU'VE EVER LISTENED to or sung the popular version of the Lord's Prayer, written by Albert Hay Malotte in 1935 and recorded by everyone from Elvis Presley to Susan Boyle to Andrea Bocelli, you know that it starts softly, almost in a whisper, "Our Father . . ." It gets a little louder with "thy kingdom come, thy will be done" and then settles into a comforting lilt for several phrases, "on earth as it is in heaven." The second half of the song then builds and builds until it explodes into the doxology, with the notes getting louder and higher. The song crescendos at "for-EHH-ver" and then ends with a slow and stately "amen."

The musical score, especially when sung well, focuses your attention on the kingdom and the power and the glory that belong to God forever and ever, and there is something very fitting about that emphasis. It reminds us to whom we are praying, about what we are praying, and the confidence we have in praying. What I like about the music—even if it is a little melodramatic—is that it reinforces the conviction, "Yes, this prayer is going to make it to the throne. Count on it: God will hear your prayer, and God will answer."

It sounds strange, but one of my biggest challenges in prayer is remembering that I am actually praying. I forget that I'm talking to the all-powerful God of the universe. I forget that I'm not just mumbling to myself. I forget that however weak my faith, God hears my prayers for Jesus's sake. The traditional ending of the Lord's Prayer helps to lift our petitions into heaven, where God will surely hear them and then respond with mercy and might, because to him belong the kingdom and the power and the glory.

One of the other benefits of the traditional ending is that it nicely bookends the Lord's Prayer. It teaches us that prayer begins and ends with the glory of God as our chief concern. It expresses confidence in God that he can do all we ask and that he is all we need. It gives voice to our belief that though the world, the flesh, and the devil may assault us, they will by no means have the final victory. Our Father in heaven is stronger than the strong man (Luke 11:21–22). All perfection belongs to God and God alone. He is a mighty and generous king, a powerful potentate, and a glorious Father without beginning or end.

And then following that final acclamation of God's glory, we seal our prayer with that little word *amen*. I had a friend in college who, in an act of quasi-rebellion, decided he would end all his prayers with "groovy" instead of "amen"—yes, this was not the 1970s but the late 1990s. He thought it was rather clever; I thought it was rather annoying. His thinking was, it's just a word to say that we're done with praying, so any old word will do. But, of course, *amen* is not just prayer-speak for *period*. Amen means "yes," "truly," or "so shall it be!" Jesus Christ is the Amen, the faithful and true witness (Rev. 3:14). In Christ we pray the Lord's Prayer with complete agreement, confidence, and hope.

But Wait

The words of the doxology provide a wonderful ending for the Lord's Prayer, and yet is the doxology actually in the Bible? The quick answer is yes and no.

The doxology is included in the King James Version but not in more recent translations such as the English Standard Version, the Christian Standard Version, or the New International Version. And there is good reason you don't see it in Matthew 6 in most English versions. The oldest and most important biblical manuscripts, which date to the fourth century, do not have the final doxology. It does not appear in the Latin Vulgate either. Likewise, the church fathers Tertullian, Cyprian, Origen, and Augustine do not show familiarity with the ending. On the other hand, the Greek father Chrysostom comments on it in his sermon on the Lord's Prayer. Moreover, the doxology is found in many ancient Greek manuscripts, as well as Syriac, Coptic, and Latin translations. In summary then, the doxology is clearly ancient, but the best and oldest manuscripts don't have it.

So are we wrong to conclude the Lord's Prayer with the traditional doxology? No, certainly not. For starters, we know that the doxology was used with the Lord's Prayer in the early church. Recall that the first-century church manual, the *Didache*, called on Christians to recite the prayer three times a day. In giving the prayer to recite, the *Didache* includes ". . . yours is the power and the glory forever" (8:2). In chapter 9 of the *Didache* the same doxology is used in what appears to be a congregational response for a Lord's Supper liturgy. It's possible that this was one of the original uses for the ending of the Lord's Prayer as well.

Moreover, in using the traditional ending, we aren't adding any ideas that weren't already present in the Lord's Prayer. The second petition mentions the kingdom. The third petition implicitly calls on God's power to incline our wills to his. And the first petition asks that God's name would be set apart and glorified in all the earth. The concluding acclamation is consistent with all that we ask for in the rest of the prayer.

The most important reason why it's not wrong to use the traditional doxology is that it has its origins in the Old Testament Scriptures. That's why I answered the question, Is it in the Bible? with yes and no. The doxology is not in Matthew 6, but it is in 1 Chronicles 29. It comes from the prayer David prayed in the assembly after the offerings for the building of the temple had been collected:

David blessed the LORD in the presence of all the assembly. And David said: "Blessed are you, O LORD, the God of Israel our father, forever and ever. Yours, O LORD, is the greatness and the power and the glory and the victory and the majesty, for all that is in the heavens and in the earth is yours. Yours is the kingdom, O LORD, and you are exalted as head above all. Both riches and honor come from you, and you rule over all. In your hand are power and might, and in your hand it is to make great and to give strength to all. And now we thank you, our God, and praise your glorious name. (1 Chron. 29:10–13)

It's a magnificent prayer, isn't it? It's easy to see how the doxology of the Lord's Prayer comes directly from David's prayer. You can even think of the traditional ending as a summary of David's longer prayer. Or, to flip it around, we can use David's prayer as an expanded version of all that we want to say in praising God for his kingdom, his power, and his glory. In fact, there may be no better way to end this final exposition, and to end this book as a whole, than by using these verses from 1 Chronicles 29 to lead us in prayer. For in praying through David's prayer, we not only pray through the ending of the Lord's Prayer; we are reminded to pray for *everything* Jesus teaches us in the Lord's Prayer.

So, with that in mind, and with the eyes of our heart toward heaven, let us pray.

———

Blessed are you, O Lord, the God of Israel our father,
> the God of Abraham, Isaac, and Jacob;
> the God who saved Moses from the Nile,
> who rescued your people from Pharaoh,
> who forgave Aaron for the golden calf,
> who delivered Jericho into the hands of Joshua;
> the God who strengthened Samson and gave courage to
>> Gideon and Jael, the wife of Heber;
> the God who showed kindness to Ruth and made Ruth so
>> kind;
> the God who cast down Eli and raised up Samuel;
> the God who rejected Saul and chose Jesse's son;

the God who gave king David a heart like yours and gave Solomon wisdom when he prayed;

the God of Elijah's guts and Elisha's miracles and Josiah's faithfulness;

the God of Job's patience, Isaiah's prophecies, and Jeremiah's lamentations;

the God who sent Israel into Babylon and promised to bring them back;

the God who promised that the valley of dry bones would live and the glory would return to the temple;

the God who saved Daniel from the Lion's den, the three men from the fiery furnace, and Gomer from herself;

the God of John the Baptist's boldness, and Paul's preaching, and Stephen's courage;

the God of Mary and Elizabeth, of Mary and Martha, of Joanna and Susanna, and of all the other godly women who loved Jesus;

the God of Peter, Andrew, James, and John, and all the other men who failed at first, but followed Christ faithfully until the end;

the God of the apostles and prophets, the saints and martyrs;

the God of rebels and reformers, and Puritans and patriarchs;

the God of electing love and second chances.

Blessed are you, O Lord, the God of Israel our Father, forever and ever.

Yours, O Lord, is the greatness—

the right to do as you please and the ability to do what
you desire.
Yours, O Lord, is the power—
the never-tiring strength to do anything and everything
consistent with your character.
Yours, O Lord, is the glory—
not to us, O Lord, not to us, but to your name be
praise.
Yours, O Lord, is the victory—
more than able to subdue our pride, break our addictions,
and conquer our children's hearts.
Yours, O Lord, is the majesty—
more stately than any castle, more regal than any palace,
more spectacular than any skyscraper. You are God and
there is no other.
All that is in the heavens and in the earth is yours.
You made the world and everything in it.
Every tree is your tree. Every mountain is your
mountain. Every title and every deed on every house
belong to you. Every retirement account belongs
to you.
You own the cattle on a thousand hills and the car in every
garage.
It is all yours.
You cannot be served by human hands as though you
needed anything, since you yourself give to all mankind
life and breath and everything.
*Yours is the kingdom, O Lord, and you are exalted as head
above all.*

You are the only King and head of the church.

We give you the final say over everything.

Let God be true and every man a liar.

We put you at the center of everything. Every sermon,
every song, every prayer, every Sunday school
class, every baptism, every birth, every death, every
marriage, every Sunday, and every week, and every
year is for you, that you would be exalted above all
things.

Both riches and honor come from you, and you rule over all.

The clothes we have. You gave them to us.

The food we eat. It's from your hand.

The roof over our head. It is a gift.

Some of us have cottages, boats, fields, land, pools,
televisions, libraries, smartphones, purses, toys, video
games, computers, vacations, and money in the bank.
What have we done to deserve so much?

Some of us have received honors, recognition, awards,
influence, prestige, and notoriety. It's all from you.

We have so much, not because we are holier than others.
But because you have blessed us so much more than we
deserve.

In your hand are power and might, and in your hand it is to
make great and to give strength to all.

You raise up kings and you tear down kingdoms.

You make presidents and you break them.

You gift pastors and you take away their gifting.

You bless churches and you close their doors.

You prosper nations and you cause them to stumble.

You alone can do all things, and in you alone do we trust.

Some trust in chariots and some trust in princes; some trust
in the government, some trust in their savings, and
some trust in themselves; but we trust in the name of
the Lord our God.

*And now we thank you, our God, and praise your glorious
name.*

We thank you, Father, for choosing us, calling us, humbling
us, converting us, justifying us, changing us, and
keeping us.

We thank you, only-begotten Son, for the mystery of your
incarnation, the suffering of your humiliation, the love
of your substitution, the victory of your resurrection,
and the glory of your exaltation.

We thank you, Holy Spirit, for giving us gifts to serve you,
voices to praise you, and hearts to love you.

We thank you for all the joys of this life—friends, family,
food, drink, work, music, stories, games, art, travel,
learning, and play.

We thank you most of all for the joys of the life to come—
an end to sin and suffering and the beginning of our
eternal praise to God and to the Lamb.

We praise you our great and glorious God:

Creator, Redeemer, Sustainer,

Judge and Deliverer,

Wonderful Counselor and Prince of Peace,

The Way, the Truth, and the Life,

Our Comforter, our Sacrifice, and our Shepherd,

Our Lord, our Savior, our Friend.

We praise you Father, Son, and Holy Spirit with one voice as
we pray the prayer Jesus taught us to pray, saying:
Our Father in heaven,
hallowed be your name.
Your kingdom come, your will be done, on earth as it is in
heaven.
Give us this day our daily bread, and forgive us our debts,
as we also have forgiven our debtors.
And lead us not into temptation,
but deliver us from evil.
For yours is the kingdom, and the power, and the glory
forever. Amen.

Study Guide

Chapter 1: When You Pray

1. Kevin begins the book with this sentence: "Is there any activity more essential to the Christian life, and yet more discouraging *in* the Christian's life, than prayer?" Why does Kevin say it? How are you encouraged by it?

2. Kevin writes, "Jesus wants to make sure we are praying for the right reasons from the right heart." What does that mean?

3. Looking at 1 Kings 18:20–40, what prayers or methods of prayer can make a Christian look like a hypocrite or a pagan?

4. How is prayer an act of faith?

5. What facets of God's character encouraged you in this chapter?

Chapter 2: Our Father

1. How does the Lord's Prayer teach us how to pray all our other prayers?

2. How do the first three requests of the prayer focus on God's glory? How do the second three focus on our good?

3. How should community prayer look, and how is that encouraging?

4. How can an awe of and an intimacy with God improve or change our prayers?

5. How does Kevin's explanation of "hallow" help you better understand prayer? Why is it important that it comes first in the Lord's Prayer?

Chapter 3: Our Desire

1. What is meant by God's kingdom and by God's will in the Lord's Prayer?

2. What are we asking for when we make the petitions "Your kingdom come, your will be done"? How should we live our lives in light of these requests?

3. Describe the difference between the kingdom and the church.

4. How does this chapter help you understand the "already and not yet" of the kingdom?

5. Explain the differences between God's will of decree, God's will of desire, and the will of direction.

Chapter 4: Our Daily Bread

1. What does focusing on each individual word of this petition, "Give us this day our daily bread," teach us about prayer?

2. Why is it important to be concerned first with God's name, God's kingdom, and God's will before asking for God to give to us?

3. How does this petition show us God's kindness?

4. In Kevin's list of reasons for why we shouldn't be anxious, which verse in Matthew 6 do you need to preach to your own heart?

5. What does "bread" encompass?

Chapter 5: Our Debts

1. Kevin defines *debts*, *trespasses*, and *sins*. How are they different, and how are Kevin's definitions helpful?

2. Forgiveness covers both our vertical relationship with God and our horizontal relationships with others. Do you find one more difficult than the other?

3. How were you helped by Kevin's explanations of what forgiveness is and what it is not?

4. In today's culture, judgment and judgmentalism are often considered the same thing. How does Kevin explain the difference?

5. What does Kevin mean when he writes that "the Bible is clear that the *unforgiving* person is an *unforgiven* person"?

Chapter 6: Our Plea

1. Why should we look at "Lead us not into temptation, but deliver us from evil" as one petition instead of two?

2. What are the different types of temptations in the Bible?

3. What were the three temptations set before Jesus, and how are they set before us today?

4. How would you answer Kevin's question, "In which room is the devil most likely to whisper in your ear?"

5. Kevin writes that we "live our lives too serious about casual things and too casual about serious things." Where do you see this in your own life?

Chapter 7: His Glory

1. What is significant about the fact that the Lord's Prayer is book-ended by the glory of God?

2. Kevin states that "one of my biggest challenges in prayer is remembering that I am actually praying." Do you resonate with that statement?

3. Kevin acknowledges that this last phrase is lacking in some of the most ancient Greek manuscripts, and yet he invites us to use it. Why can we feel confident including it when we pray the prayer?

4. How does Kevin's prayer increase your confidence to pray?

5. Which of God's names would you like to understand further, and why?

Notes

Chapter 1: When You Pray

1. See Charles M. Laymon, *The Lord's Prayer in Its Biblical Setting* (Nashville, TN: Abingdon, 1968), 32–48.
2. See David Instone-Brewer, "The Eighteen Benedictions and the Minim before 70 CE," *Journal of Theological Studies* 54 (April 2003): 25–44.
3. John Stott, *The Message of the Sermon on the Mount* (Downers Grove, IL: IVP Academic, 1978), 144.

Chapter 2: Our Father

1. Cyprian of Carthage, "On the Lord's Prayer," in *Fathers of the Third Century: Hippolytus, Cyprian, Novatian, Appendix*, ed. Alexander Roberts, James Donaldson, and A. Cleveland Coxe, trans. Robert Ernest Wallis, vol. 5, The Ante-Nicene Fathers (Buffalo, NY: Christian Literature Co., 1886), 448.
2. Martin Luther, *The Sermon on the Mount (Sermons) and the Magnificat*, ed. Jaroslav Pelikan, vol. 21, Luther's Works (St. Louis, MO: Concordia, 1956), 146.
3. John Calvin, *Institutes of the Christian Religion*, ed. John T. McNeil, trans. Ford L. Battles (Philadelphia: Westminster Press, 1960), 3.20.34.
4. Charles M. Laymon, *The Lord's Prayer in Its Biblical Setting* (Nashville, TN: Abingdon: 1968), 85.
5. J. I. Packer, *Praying the Lord's Prayer* (Wheaton, IL: Crossway, 2007), 35.
6. Calvin, *Institutes*, 3.20.41.

Chapter 3: Our Desire

1. Andrew Roberts, *Churchill: Walking with Destiny* (New York: Penguin, 2018), 39–40.

2. D. A. Carson, "Matthew," in *The Expositor's Bible Commentary: Matthew, Mark, Luke,* ed. Frank E. Gaebelein, vol. 8 (Grand Rapids, MI: Zondervan, 1984), 170.

3. See George E. Ladd, *A Theology of the New Testament,* rev. ed. (Grand Rapids, MI: Eerdmans, 1993), 101–2.

4. J. I. Packer, *Praying the Lord's Prayer* (Wheaton, IL: Crossway, 2007), 53.

5. Darrell L. Bock, *Acts,* Baker Exegetical Commentary on the New Testament (Grand Rapids, MI: Baker Academic, 2007), 60.

Chapter 4: Our Daily Bread

1. The Greek word *epiousios* is found in the Bible only in verse 11 and later in Luke's version of the Lord's Prayer in Luke 11:3. The word has been subject to many translation theories, some quite ingeniuous. Some think the etymology of the word suggests the translation "for tomorrow" (see the footnote in the ESV). The basic meaning of *epiousios* implies "for what follows," meaning, in the morning, for the coming day, or at night, for the day next. In either case, "daily" is an appropriate translation and is supported by virtually every English translation.

2. Herman Witsius, *Sacred Dissertations on the Lord's Prayer* (Grand Rapids, MI: Reformation Heritage, 2010), 298, 300. Witsius also notes that in addition to industry and justice, "our bread" teaches us "the duty of depending on the favor of God" (301), but since I mentioned this idea earlier, I did not include his third point in my explanation of "our."

3. "Daily bread is put either for all those things which meet the wants of this life, in reference to which He says in His teaching, 'Take no thought for the morrow:' so that on this account there is added, 'Give us this day:' or, it is put for the sacrament of the body of Christ, which we daily receive: or, for the spiritual food, of which the same Lord says, 'Labour for the meat which perisheth not;' and again, 'I am the bread of life, which came down from heaven.'" See, Augustine of Hippo, "Our Lord's Sermon on the Mount," in *Saint Augustin: Sermon on the Mount, Harmony of the Gospels, Homilies on the Gospels,* ed. Philip Schaff, trans. William Findlay and David Schley Schaff,

vol. 6, A Select Library of the Nicene and Post-Nicene Fathers of the Christian Church, First Series (New York: Christian Literature Company, 1888), 41.

4. "Give Me Jesus," Afro-American spiritual, n.d.

5. Richard Coekin, *Our Father: Enjoying God in Prayer* (Nottingham, UK: Inter-Varsity Press, 2009), 114.

6. Annie S. Hawks, "I Need Thee Every Hour," 1872.

Chapter 5: Our Debts

1. Herman Witsius, *Sacred Dissertations on the Lord's Prayer* (Grand Rapids, MI: Reformation Heritage, 2010), 313. For ease of reading, I slightly altered the punctuation in the quotation.

2. Zacharias Ursinus and G. W. Williard, *The Commentary of Dr. Zacharias Ursinus on the Heidelberg Catechism* (Cincinnati, OH: Elm Street Printing, 1888), 652.

3. Thomas Watson, *Body of Divinity* (1992; repr., Grand Rapids, MI: Baker, 1979), 581.

4. Chris Brauns, *Unpacking Forgiveness: Biblical Answers for Complex Questions and Deep Wounds* (Wheaton, IL: Crossway, 2008).

5. Kevin DeYoung, "Following Up on Forgiveness," The Gospel Coalition, February 13, 2014, https://www.thegospelcoalition.org. The interview first appeared on my blog April 7, 2009. The Calvin reference is from John Calvin, *Institutes of the Christian Religion*, ed. John T. McNeil, trans. Ford Lewis Battles (Philadelphia: Westminster Press, 1960), 3.3.19.

6. Mel Gibson, dir., *Braveheart* (Los Angeles: Paramount Pictures Studios, 1995).

7. Witsius, *Sacred Dissertations*, 323.

Chapter 6: Our Plea

1. Herman Witsius, *Sacred Dissertations on the Lord's Prayer* (Grand Rapids, MI: Reformation Heritage, 2010), 342.

General Index

Scripture Index

Also Available from Kevin DeYoung

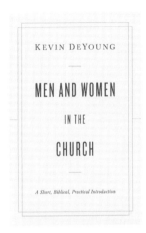

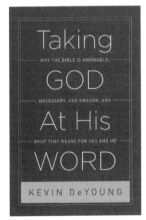

For more information, visit **crossway.org**.